THE LEGEND OF
BRINK'S

*This book is dedicated to the men and women
of the Brink's uniform who've given their lives to
safeguard the valuables entrusted to their care
and to protect those around them.*

THE LEGEND OF
BRINK'S

JEFFREY L. RODENGEN

Edited by Elizabeth Fernandez
Design and layout by Sandy Cruz

Write Stuff Enterprises, Inc.
1001 South Andrews Avenue
Fort Lauderdale, FL 33316
1-800-900-Book (1-800-900-2665)
(954) 462-6657
www.writestuffbooks.com

The publisher has made every effort to identify and locate the source of the photographs included in this edition of *The Legend of Brink's*. Grateful acknowledgment is made to those who have kindly granted permission for the use of their materials in this edition. If there are instances where proper credit was not given, the publisher will gladly make any necessary corrections in subsequent printings.

Publisher's Cataloging in Publication
(Prepared by The Donohue Group, Inc.)

Rodengen, Jeffrey L.
    The legend of Brink's / Jeffrey L. Rodengen ; edited by Elizabeth Fernandez ; design and layout by Sandy Cruz ; [foreword by John W. Snow].

    p. : ill. ; cm.

    Includes bibliographical references and index.
    ISBN-13: 978-1-932022-39-1
    ISBN-10: 1-932022-39-2

1. Brinks, Inc.—History. 2. Private security services—United States—History. I. Fernandez, Elizabeth. II. Cruz, Sandy. III. Snow, John W. IV. Title.

HV8291.U6- R634 2009
368.28   2009925413

Completely produced in the United States of America
1 3 5 7 9 10 8 6 4 2

TABLE OF CONTENTS

FOREWORD

BY

JOHN W. SNOW

FORMER SECRETARY OF THE TREASURY OF THE UNITED STATES OF AMERICA

I FIRST CAME TO TRULY APPRECIate Brink's as a young attorney working in Washington, D.C., where I represented Brink's on a variety of matters before the Interstate Commerce Commission (ICC), including applications to the ICC for licenses of public convenience and necessity. Subsequently, I was pleased to have been at the forefront of efforts to deregulate the trucking, railroad, and aviation industries. When that happened, a new day dawned and Brink's was among the few major transportation companies capable of successfully making the transition to a deregulated, highly competitive environment. Brink's excelled at understanding this new world and continued to thrive with a renewed emphasis on service, competitiveness, and getting the underlying metrics of the business lined up right.

When I became Secretary of the Treasury, I worked closely with the U.S. Mint and Bureau of Engraving and Printing in overseeing the integrity of the U.S. currency. Brink's proved an extraordinary partner in these efforts and has long been at the forefront of providing services to move the coin and currency of the country from the printing presses and mints to the Federal Reserve banks and throughout the banking system. U.S. currency and coin must be moved safely with a great degree of reliability, ensuring that it gets where it needs to be to serve the nation's economy. The services that Brink's provides the Treasury and the Federal Reserve remain a fundamental element in the integrity of the U.S. monetary system. In an even broader perspective, Brink's has an integral role in the way the financial system of the United States, and the world, works. Since bills and currency are the lifeblood of the economy, Brink's employees play a critically important role. They do it unobtrusively. They do it without incident. They do it seamlessly.

Brink's continues to stand out because of its deep and solid corporate culture. The company remains strongly committed to the safety of its employees and the security of all cargo in its responsible charge. Brink's believes in the classic adage that employees are by far the company's most important assets. That belief has helped Brink's survive for a remarkable 150 years. The company takes its culture seriously, and its underlying values have proven essential for its success.

Another measure of the success of an organization is its safety record. A safety record reveals what you care about—what you value. Business school studies have confirmed a very high correlation between safety and success in other dimensions of performance. If you believe in safety, you believe in your people. If you treat your people well, you engineer your company to work the right way. For nearly 20 years, I was privileged to hold leadership positions at CSX Corporation. During my tenure, I learned much about the ability of culture and leadership to forge creative and strategic solutions to successfully achieve goals. Brink's has been blessed with 150 years of energized leadership, continued today with proprietary solutions and a truly global presence under CEO Michael Dan.

Congratulations to all of the men and women who have made Brink's one of the world's most trusted brands. Trust, integrity, safety. And now 150 years of success. It just doesn't get much better than that.

JOHN W. SNOW SERVED AS THE 73ᴿᴰ SECRETARY of the Treasury from 2003 to 2006. He has a long history of working in the transportation industry, including 20 years at CSX Corporation, where he was chairman and CEO for more than a decade. Mr. Snow also served as Chairman of the Business Roundtable, a group comprised of 250 CEOs from the most influential companies in the United States. His dedication to government service included a number of years in the Department of Transportation in the early 1970s, where he held numerous key posts, including Deputy Undersecretary, Administrator of the National Highway Safety Administration, Assistant Secretary for Governmental Affairs, and Deputy Assistant Secretary for Policy, Plans, and International Affairs. Additionally, Mr. Snow served as Co-Chair of the Conference Board's Blue Ribbon Commission on Public Trust and Private Enterprise, Co-Chair of the National Commission on Financial Institution Reform, Recovery, and Enforcement, and on the National Commission on Economic Growth and Tax Reform.

ACKNOWLEDGMENTS

MANY DEDICATED PEOPLE ASSISTED IN THE research, preparation, and publication of *The Legend of Brink's.*

The development of historical timelines and the principal archival research was completed by Laura Putre, while Senior Editor Elizabeth Fernandez managed the editorial content. Vice President/ Creative Director Sandy Cruz brought the story to life. The author is especially grateful to John W. Snow for contributing the book's foreword.

Several key individuals associated with Brink's provided their assistance in the development of the book from its outline to its finished product. Compiling the vast amounts of information and images necessary for a project of this magnitude would not have been possible without the assistance of many people. Individuals who assisted with the collection of historic research and photographic materials include David Kapella, curator of The Brink's Museum; Glenn Humphreys, director of the special collections reading room at the Chicago Public Library; and Julie Lynch, librarian at the Historical Room of the Conrad Sulzer Library.

All of the people interviewed—Brink's employees, retirees, and friends—were generous with their time and insights.

Special thanks are due to all Brink's employees, past and present. Together, they have ensured that the Brink's name will always be synonymous with safety and security.

Grateful acknowledgement is especially due to the courageous, dedicated Brink's employees who have lost their lives in the line of duty. Since the company's inception, Brink's employees have always risked their lives to get the job done, banding together to selflessly protect life and property. Their devotion, bravery, and sacrifice in the face of danger will never be forgotten.

Washington Perry Brink, known as Perry to his family and friends, founded his express business on Randolph Street in Chicago. The area served as a bustling center for wholesalers and hauling companies, close to both the river and the city's Central Business District. *(Photo courtesy of Chicago History Museum #ICHi-31327. Photographer—John W. Taylor.)*

CHAPTER ONE

BRINK'S CITY EXPRESS

THE EARLY YEARS

To step on the sidewalks of 19th-century Chicago was to become part of a bustling, no-holds-barred burg on the verge of greatness. A cow town knee deep in mud, the city burst at the seams with new people and new opportunities.

—Historian Theodore J. Karamanski[1]

IN THE 1850s, DURING THE HEIGHT of the Gold Rush era, when bandits roamed the frontier looking for cargo wagons to rob, firms began offering cross-country insured delivery for all money and valuables shipped back East.[2] Cross-country delivery outfits established themselves as bastions of order and security amid the chaos and lawlessness of the Wild West. Washington Perry Brink, known to family and friends as Perry, was impressed by the success of these firms.[3]

Perry suffered a financial setback in 1855 when the farm he had purchased from his wife Fidelia's brother fell into foreclosure.[4] The bustling city of Chicago, a former prairie fort, teemed with possibility—a place where anyone with enough ambition, creativity, and perseverance could accomplish great things. Sensing the opportunity, Perry, along with his wife and his three-year-old son Arthur Perry, moved to Chicago in 1859. Perry had a new niche in mind—delivery services within the city limits of Chicago.

Chicago's Innovative Attitude

In the 26 years since its incorporation in 1837, Chicago's population had grown from a smattering of spirited settlers to a bustling city of approximately 95,000, not counting visiting tourists, wholesale buyers, salesmen, bankers, and financiers. With a Lake Michigan port and railroads fanning out in three directions, Chicago already boasted more than 60 hotels, 56 churches, and 80 ballrooms.[5] The construction of the Illinois and Michigan Canal in 1848, linking the Illinois River with Lake Michigan, positioned Chicago to become the trade center to the West. The Illinois Central Railroad launched the city's first regular rail service in the 1850s, introducing a route that traveled from Chicago in the north to the Mississippi River port of Cairo, Illinois, in the south. Rail expansion boomed, with the first all-rail link established between Chicago and New York City in 1858.

The fact that Chicago served as a burgeoning rail center made it an ideal location for a local express company. The railroads brought cargo into town, but it was up to smaller companies to make deliveries from the railroad depot. The much-improved roads added to the appeal. In the 1850s, it had been tough going for horse-and-wagon operators, because, at the time, Chicago's streets were either unpaved or covered with wooden planks. Plank roads, introduced in the 1840s, were considered a step up from the dirt roads common at the

Only one photo of Perry has survived to this day. He is shown here with his wife, Fidelia. *(Photo courtesy of Brink's Museum.)*

time, and tolls were charged to use them. The improvements in plank roads contributed to the growth of express services in Chicago, and by 1848, 200 wagons per day were coming into the city, most opting to pay tolls.

Another innovation came when the first section of Nicholson Pavement was installed. This road surface, which originated in Chicago, consisted of pine blocks dipped in tar and laid like bricks. Pitch was poured over that, and then the road was covered in a layer of gravel. A visitor to Chicago at the time called this "the *ne plus ultra* of comfort for horse and rider, for passersby and ladies living near."[6] It would soon become common on main streets, both in Chicago and elsewhere.

Unfortunately, wagon drivers still had to contend with constant flooding, as the streets had been laid only slightly above the water level. City officials recognized that something had to be done. "The alternatives seemed grim," wrote authors Harold M. Mayer and Richard C. Wade in *Chicago: Growth of a Metropolis.* "Either put up perpetually with the inconveniences or pull down the city, raise its grade level, and rebuild. Yet another possibility remained—contrive a way to hoist up the city itself. As outlandish as it seemed to some, Chicago chose the most difficult policy."[7]

In 1855, the city began raising its streets, a process that would continue for the next 20 years. Buildings were lifted on jacks and new paving and drainage systems were installed. David McRae, a British citizen visiting Chicago, recalled a surprising moment that typified the city's attitude toward innovation:

The Briggs House, a gigantic hotel five stories high, solid masonry weighing 22 tons, was raised four-and-a-half feet, and new foundations built below. The people were in it all the time—coming and going, eating and sleeping—the whole business of the hotel proceeding without interruption. ... Never a day passed that I did not meet one or

1854

Early express companies such as Wells Fargo and Adams Express inspire Washington Perry Brink to start his own express delivery service.

CHICAGO HISTORY MUSEUM #ICHi-20543

1859

Perry opens Brink's City Express in Chicago after purchasing a single wagon.

BRINK'S MUSEUM

1855

The growth of the railroad turns Chicago into the manufacturing center of the Midwest, bringing in travelers that needed luggage and parcels shipped from the depot to their hotels and places of business.

CHICAGO HISTORY MUSEUM #ICHi-23059

Remarkably, Chicago residents went about their daily business uninterrupted as workers raised streets and buildings in an effort to control flooding. *(Lithograph courtesy of Chicago History Museum #ICHi-00698.)*

more houses shifting their quarters. One day I met nine.

Going out Great Madison Street in the horsecars, we had to stop twice to let houses get across. [A shop rolled by, and] as it moved along, the shopkeeper stood leaning against the doorpost, smoking a cigar.[8]

Brink's City Express

Drawn by the very same innovative attitude that made Chicago a success, Perry purchased a horse-drawn delivery wagon in 1859 for between $100 and $200 to make deliveries of parcels, baggage, and merchandise within the city limits.[9]

When he embarked on his first delivery on May 5 of that year, the wagon bore his new company's name—Brink's City Express. It was a modest beginning for what would one day become a multi-billion-dollar global company.

According to *Brink's—The Money Movers: The Story of a Century of Service* by R. A. Seng and J. V. Gilmour, Perry started out transporting "trunks and

LIBRARY OF CONGRESS #LC-DIG-PPMSCA-19442

1871

Some 18,000 buildings are consumed in the Great Chicago Fire. Brink's Express loses its headquarters, but not its horses and wagons, and is back up and running within a week.

CHICAGO PUBLIC LIBRARY, SPECIAL COLLECTIONS AND PRESERVATION DIVISION, CCW 5.79

1860

Brink's employees deliver luggage and parcels during the Republican National Convention, where an estimated 50,000 out-of-town delegates and spectators assemble to watch dark-horse candidate Abraham Lincoln win the nomination over William Seward, the favored contender.

carpet bags, traveling boxes and sample cases," and even did "light draying for the merchants in town."[10]

In 1860, delegates from all over the country descended on Chicago for the Republican National Convention. Up to 50,000 people visited Chicago to take part in the historic event and help shape the party's future.[11] The event proved fortuitous for Brink's, as the fledgling company was chosen to help deliver parcels and transport luggage for delegates from the train station to the luxurious Richmond Hotel, where the New York delegation under "hardball" party boss Thurlow Weed had set up camp.[12] In a single day, the Illinois Central Railroad—just one of a dozen railways in the city by that time—brought in 12,000 people.[13] The city's hotels were filled, sometimes five or six to a room, and some weary travelers even resorted to sleeping on billiard tables in taverns. The event itself was held in a massive wood-frame building known as the Wigwam, located at the corner of Lake and Market streets. Party contractors erected the structure in just five weeks. Billed as the

Built in five weeks and seating 12,000, the Wigwam at Lake and Market streets was the site of the historic 1860 Republican National Convention. *(Lithograph courtesy of Chicago History Museum #ICHi-26089. Creator—Chas. Shober.)*

largest auditorium in the United States at the time, it measured 100 feet by 180 feet, seated 12,000, and cost a mere $5,000 to build.[14] Dark-horse candidate Abraham Lincoln, who had not held office in a dozen years, won over favored nominee William Seward from New York in a boisterous, nail-biting upset that took three ballots to decide.[15]

Attracting Customers

By April 30, 1868, Brink's had begun running classified ads in the *Chicago Tribune*, one of the city's major newspapers. "Wanted—By Brink's City Express, 119 Randolph Street," the first one read. "Two good horses to work single, to be sound and kind and weigh not less than 1,100 pounds."[16] By this time, according to early advertisements, Brink's delivery wagons were making "three trips per day to and from each division of the city" at 10 A.M. and 5 P.M., transporting "packages, baggage, and light freight." Trunks and luggage cost 25 cents to ship for one piece, 40 cents for two, 50 cents for three, and "other goods in proportion."[17] Barrels of flour and small packages also cost 25 cents a piece.[18]

Perry and his family lived at 119 Randolph Street and for a time ran the company out of their home. By 1870, Brink's headquarters had moved to a separate office nearby at 37 Randolph Street.[19]

An Early Focus on Safety

IN THE BEGINNING, BRINK'S DELIVERIES WERE MADE in unassuming open-air, one-horse buggies designed to blend in with the thousands of other buggies traversing Chicago's city streets. According to W. B. Wyne, an early employee of Brink's who later became vice president and treasurer, inconspicuousness worked to the company's advantage at the time, since deliverymen, if spotted, made easy targets for robbers. They often traveled alone and carried only a single small revolver, hidden under the buggy seat, that they took with them on deliveries. "Our dependence for safety was not on the gun but the manner in which we did our work," Wyne explained.[1]

Wyne recalled carrying the $10,000 payroll for the University of Chicago, an early customer, wrapped in newspaper to give would-be robbers "the impression that the package was of small value."[2]

However, as the country began to transition from coins to lighter, more compact paper currency, the amount of money moved daily in cities such as Chicago increased exponentially. "This caused the eyes of outlaws to turn from the open country of the far West to larger cities, and ban-

In the early days, Brink's messengers carried payroll deliveries for customers such as the University of Chicago in plain newspaper wrapping to avoid attracting attention. *(Photo courtesy of Brink's Museum.)*

dit activities shifted to the large centers of population and wealth," wrote Forrest Crissey in *Moving Money*.[3]

Brink's men began traveling in pairs. One driver preferred a dog as protection, so an English bulldog went on the payroll at $3 a week.[4]

Once in its new headquarters, Brink's devised a unique way of communicating with its customers in the area. The new location also served as the communications hub of the company. Customers wrote their delivery requests on a blackboard out front.[20]

Tough and Tenacious

At first, Perry hired only single men, reasoning that without family obligations, they would be willing to work longer, more erratic hours. Concerned for their safety, Perry expected his employees to board with him so they would be easily available for customer deliveries.[21]

Early employees were generally tough, strong, and tenacious. Unlike modern Brink's applicants, who undergo extensive background checks, Perry's employees were hired on the basis of word of mouth, appearance, and bearing.[22] Deliverymen often carried heavy bags full of gold and silver coins as part of their job, since payroll currency was not widely used at the time. They trained by running informal contests to test their strength, such as lifting beer wagons and whiskey barrels.[23] The standard wage reached approximately $12 a week, though key deliverymen could make as much as $18.[24]

Since the early days, Brink's workforce has been noted for its bravery. A *Tribune* article described a Brink's driver rescuing a family from a rabid dog. According to the story, the "raving yellow cur" tried to enter the Modjeski residence but was captured in the home's vestibule by quick-thinking Mrs. Modjeski. Several neighbors attempted to subdue the dog and failed.

"It is hard to say how the siege would have ended if Ole Hanson, a sturdy Swedish driver for Brink's Express, had not happened along," stated the article. "Ole stopped to find out what the trouble was, and when told of the perilous situation smiled and volunteered to annihilate the dog." Grabbing an iron bar from his wagon, Hanson "advanced boldly into the vestibule. The dog sprang at Hanson with wide open and foaming mouth," but with a single blow the driver "knocked him senseless."[25]

Brink's on Fire

By 1871, Perry had begun expanding his wagon fleet. According to an 1871 ad, "Having recently added more teams to our already large business of some five years' growth, we are better prepared than ever to transport baggage and merchandise to and from all parts of the city."[26]

Perry worked hard to offer promotions and seek partnerships that would benefit his business. In 1871, Perry struck an arrangement with some railroads to sell train tickets and shuttle passengers' luggage, according to an ad, "free of expense to the Michigan Central and Michigan Southern Railroads on all tickets purchased at our office to go east of Buffalo. All other merchandise will be taken at one-half the usual rates to any part of the city."

Perry soon added Illinois Central, Pittsburgh, and Fort Wayne railroads to his baggage service.[27] However, just as Brink's had begun to prosper, the company faced disaster.

On October 8, 1871, a barn owned by the O'Leary family on DeKoven Street caught fire a few minutes past 9 P.M. It had been an especially dry year, and the fire quickly spread, consuming the working-class neighborhood's wood-frame houses. "The fire department, exhausted from a large and costly fire that had wiped out four square blocks the day before, could not get equipment to the scene fast enough," wrote Mayer and Wade in *Chicago: Growth of a Metropolis*. "Within minutes, the blaze was out of control."[28]

It coursed through the city's Near West Side, then jumped the river's south branch at Van Buren Street. Burning an average of 65 acres per hour, it hit the city's waterworks engine house, cutting off

PERRY'S MYSTERIOUS PARTNERS

RECORDS SHOW THAT PERRY BRINK ACTUALLY had two partners in the early days of Brink's City Express, although little is known about either of them. In 1870, the Chicago City Directory lists M. T. Stiles as coproprietor of Brink's, and an 1870 *Chicago Tribune* advertisement lists Stiles as a partner.[1] Any other records mentioning Stiles or describing what part he played in Brink's early growth have been lost.

More information exists regarding Perry's second partner, Otto Moor, whose name appears in Brink's ads from 1871 to 1872.[2] He hailed from Vermont, Perry's home state, and moved to Chicago in 1865, where he served as a senior partner in A. M. Moor and Bro., a family firm.

By 1873, Moor had left Brink's to strike out on his own. An ad for Moor's City Express in the *Chicago Tribune* described its "exclusive delivery of American Merchants Union Express Co.'s goods," and mentioned that it was "also connected with Oak Park, Evanston, and other outside express companies."[3]

According to his 1880 obituary in the *Tribune*, Moor died at age 58 of heart disease.[4]

the water supply. Even buildings thought fireproof, such as the opulent *Chicago Tribune* building and Marshall Field's department store, were left charred husks.

"Almost nothing was overlooked," wrote Mayer and Wade. "Wooden houses, commercial and industrial buildings, private mansions, and even markers in the cemetery were consumed before the lake confined the blaze."[29]

The fire finally died out after three days, destroying approximately 18,000 buildings in a 3-square-mile area of the central city. Total damage estimates reached $200 million in 1871. Perry's boarding house and his Randolph Street office were completely destroyed, but according to authors R. A. Seng and J. V. Gilmour in *Brink's—The Money Movers*, Brink's employees braved the fire, using the company's own horses and wagons "to carry furniture beyond the reach of the flames."[30]

Rather than give up and leave the charred remains, the city's residents responded with a powerful combination of characteristic Midwestern bravado and big-city vision. "Within a day, John McKnight had a fruit and cider stand ready amidst the rubble of Clark Street," Mayer and Wade wrote.

Left: This Currier & Ives lithograph shows the terrified masses crossing the Randolph Street Bridge to escape the burning city. *(Lithograph courtesy of Chicago History Museum #ICHi-23436. Creator—Currier & Ives.)*

Right: No photos of the fire itself exist because the fragile photographic equipment of the day could not withstand the intense heat. This photo by an unknown observer shows the immediate aftermath of the fire, with only a few shells of buildings left standing among the ruins. *(Photo courtesy of Chicago Public Library, Special Collections and Preservation Division, ECC 1.196b.)*

"Two days later, W. D. Kerfoot, a realtor, announced he was reopening with 'all gone but wife, children, and energy.'"

Just a week after the fire, 5,497 temporary structures had been set up, and 200 permanent buildings were in the process of being rebuilt.[31] Brink's stepped up to the challenge, continuing to offer its services as the city rebuilt. According to an October 17, 1871, advertisement, "Brink's City Express will be found at Old Stand to do business at old prices."[32]

Arthur Perry Brink, a longtime horse enthusiast, would serve as vice president of the company his father Perry Brink founded. *(Photo courtesy of Brink's Museum.)*

CHAPTER TWO

GROWTH AMID MISFORTUNE

1871–1900

In the midst of a calamity without parallel in the world's history, looking upon the ashes of 30 years' accumulations, the people of this once beautiful city have resolved that CHICAGO SHALL RISE AGAIN.

—*Chicago Tribune*, October 11, 1871[1]

THE CITY BEGAN REBUILDING EVEN as the Great Chicago Fire smoldered. Railroads recovered quickly, and business continued at the Union Stockyards southwest of downtown, which escaped the worst of the fire. Months earlier, The McCormick Harvesting Machine Company, a major employer in the area, had planned to move from its downtown location to a larger piece of land along the South Branch of the Chicago River. The fire hastened the move, and the new plant was up and running by February 1873.[2]

The city continued growing as it rose from the ruins. More rails were laid in 1872 than in any of the previous 10 years. From 1870 to 1872, the number of hogs in the Union Stockyards doubled. By 1873, 50 percent more grain was coming into Chicago than in 1869.[3]

Brink's City Express prospered as the city grew. "We are now running 16 teams to every division of the city, three times each day," announced an April 1872 classified ad.

Teams also made trips to the stockyards and the growing South Side townships of Hyde Park and Englewood at least once each day—twice on busy days.[4] By August 1872, Perry Brink had 20 teams and had expanded to include a new route to the prosperous West Side suburb of Riverside.[5] The exclusive suburb along the Des Plaines River

was an important stop on the Chicago, Burlington and Quincy Railroad. Its expansive streets and picturesque parks were laid out by Frederick Law Olmsted, already renowned for designing New York City's Central Park.[6]

As Brink's grew, the company's competitive prices proved key to its success. Brink's advertisements boasted of fees "one half or less the usual price charged by the other expresses," and that it was still charging its "old price" of 25 cents for a trunk "delivered from all depots to any part of the city." Founder Perry Brink also focused on expanding the company's services, offering "large wagons for moving household goods, from 75 cents to $1 per hour," according to advertisements.[7]

At the same time, Brink's struck up a partnership with American Express to collect and deliver its goods to and from train depots for customers outside the Central Business District.[8] As advertised, American Express customers who shipped "light packages" to Chicago received a

View of the 1893 World's Columbian Exposition's Festival Hall from the Grand Basin in Chicago. *(Photo courtesy of Chicago History Museum #ICHi-25052.)*

40 percent discount on local delivery through Brink's "by marking them to the care of Brink's City Express."[9]

This marked the beginning of Brink's long-term relationship with several national express companies. Over the next 40 years, Brink's would participate in numerous agreements, providing local delivery service from Chicago's railway stations. Executives from American Express and United States Express would go on to hold seats on Brink's board of directors.

A New Era

By August 1872, Brink's had begun to welcome customers from failing delivery companies such as Garden City and White's Express.[10] Thanks to thoughtful, well-timed business decisions over the years, the company continued to thrive as competitors faltered. It had become a well-oiled machine that would continue to grow and prosper even after

Perry Brink died unexpectedly of encephalitis on July 23, 1874, at the age of 43.

Perry left behind an estate valued at just under $2,654 to his wife and two children, as well as an enduring local legacy.[11] In 15 years, he had built a thriving business with little more than a good idea and assembled a loyal, knowledgeable staff that ensured the company would outlive him. According to his obituary:

> *He started in the express business, his sole capital being one wagon and his own energy. The cheapness of his charges, the conveniences he offered the public, and his own fair dealing and industry contributed to build up a large and invaluable business, and by the time of his death the [Brink's] City Express had become one of the most popular of Chicago institutions.*[12]

After Perry's death, his son Arthur Perry Brink took over the responsibilities of running the busi-

1874
Arthur Perry Brink helps manage the company after his father, Perry, dies unexpectedly.

BRINK'S MUSEUM

1879
Brink's offers its first shares of capital stock to four subscribers.

BRINK'S MUSEUM

1878
Brink's becomes one of the first businesses in Chicago with telephone service.

BRINK'S MUSEUM

Arthur Perry Brink helped run Brink's City Express after his father Perry died in 1874. *(Photo courtesy of Brink's Museum.)*

ness. Only 19 years old when his father died, Arthur had been with the company for one year and was described as a "capable and farsighted businessman" by R. A. Seng and J. V. Gilmour in *Brink's—The Money Movers: The Story of a Century of Service.*

"His associates of later years describe him as brisk, lively, and energetic," Seng and Gilmour wrote. "He believed that Brink's City Express had a bright future which could be achieved more rapidly by incorporating the company, strengthening its financial position, and interesting men of influence in the business."[13]

Leaders at Home and Away

For the next few years, the business continued to grow as Brink's acquired competitor George French's City Limits Express in 1875.[14] Brink's continued as a private company run by Arthur and businessman Julius J. Luther. Luther is mentioned

• 1893

Brink's is selected as the official transporter of money and express packages for the 1893 World's Columbian Exposition.

CHICAGO PUBLIC LIBRARY, SPECIAL COLLECTIONS AND PRESERVATION DIVISION, CDA VOL. 5, #70

MOVING MONEY

• 1891

Brink's offers its first payroll delivery.

in company records as a Brink's partner and also served as treasurer during his tenure with the company.

Meanwhile, developments in Chicago's workforce occurred that would soon have an effect on Brink's staff, as well as the entire U.S. labor force. With workers earning increasingly low wages amid grueling working conditions in many industries, the labor movement began picking up steam. In 1877, Chicago railroad, meatpacking, and lumber workers walked off the job in

YOU WILL BE SURPRISED

how quickly BRINK'S relieves you of all your baggage troubles. Just call them up and see.

They have a General Package and Baggage Delivery to all parts of the city and suburbs -- and best of all they have a switchboard with two operators.

BRINK'S C. C. EXPRESS CO.

84 Washington Street - 132-138 W. Monroe St.

TELEPHONE MONROE 109

A. P. BRINK, Manager   -   -   W. B. WYNE, Supt.

support of the Baltimore and Ohio Railroad strike in West Virginia—the nation's first labor uprising. Clashes between management and workers grew increasingly violent in Chicago, and the U.S. Army Infantry was called in. The incident raised awareness of labor issues, including the need for better wages and shorter, eight-hour workdays.[15]

The city also experienced other forms of growth and development. The first telephone service arrived in Chicago in 1877, and by 1878, the phone began to replace Brink's blackboard as the preferred means of communication between customers and messengers.[16] Brink's Express is listed in the Bell Telephone Company's November 1878 Chicago Telephone Exchange Directory as one of only 500 telephone subscribers in the city.[17]

By 1879, Brink's was doing well enough to attract outside investors to finance its further expansion. On February 28 of that year, Brink's appointed commissioners "to open books of subscription to the capital stock," according to Forrest Crissey in *Moving Money*.[18] The company also officially changed its name to Brink's Chicago City Express.

The first stockholders were Arthur Brink, Julius J. Luther, Byron Schermerhorn, and J. H. Bradley.[19] Each man bought 20 shares at $100 each for a total of $8,000 in capital. The first regular stockholders' meeting was held on March 21, 1879, at 89 Washington Street.[20]

Schermerhorn worked as an assistant agent for United States Express Company, and Bradley served as a superintendent for American Express Company. According to Seng and Gilmour, American Express and United States Express operated "over thousands of miles of railways ... but deliveries in Chicago by such inter-city agencies were limited to the downtown district," unlike Brink's, which could deliver in "outlying city and suburban areas." Owning a stake in Brink's allowed national express companies to extend their coverage, structuring local routes to fit their needs.[21]

By the 1890s, Brink's had its own switchboard and employed two switchboard operators. *(Photo courtesy of Brink's Museum.)*

Street, but by 1882 he had begun living full time in Kansas City, Missouri.[23] He was a good friend of Fred Harvey—a railroad man who started the Harvey House restaurant chain in 1875 along the Santa Fe Line—and became a partner in that business as well. The two men were so close that Harvey named his own son Byron Schermerhorn Harvey.[24]

In 1886, Bradley took over the Brink's presidency, a position he held until 1919, when he resigned because he opposed expanding the business beyond Chicago.[25] Bradley also ran Brink's from a distance. He had a home in Hinsdale, Illinois,

Left: Byron Schermerhorn served as a Union Army officer in the Civil War, was one of Brink's first stockholders, and became the company's first president after it was incorporated in 1879. *(Photo courtesy of Brink's Museum.)*

Below: J. H. Bradley, an agent for American Express, was another early stockholder and served as Brink's second president. *(Illustration courtesy of Brink's Museum.)*

Schermerhorn was named president of the company—a title neither Perry nor Arthur had previously held, "largely because the company went unincorporated for two decades after it was established in 1859," according to a 2001 article in *Brink's Link* magazine. Arthur became Brink's vice president.

Born in 1836, Schermerhorn was 20 years older than Arthur and wrote sentimental poetry as a hobby. He was a captain in the Union Army during the Civil War, and, according to the U.S. Civil War registry, he provided an important piece of intelligence to Union Commander George B. McClellan, reporting on the location of the main rebel army, its plans to march to Washington, D.C., the location of its wagon train, and its abundance of rations and artillery.[22]

Schermerhorn held the Brink's presidency from 1879 to 1886, but he was not involved in the company's day-to-day operations. In 1881, he was listed as having a home in Chicago at 3532 South LaSalle

STAMPED, SEALED, AND DELIVERED

IN THE MID-1880s, BRINK'S BEGAN ISSUING ITS OWN stamps. The earliest version, affixed to packages up to 15 pounds, featured an evocative black-and-white line drawing of a "lone expressman" driving a classic Brink's light delivery wagon. Stamps were placed on the outside of trunks and parcels to prove that customers had prepaid the delivery fee. They were denominated by weight, not price, so they could still be used if Brink's changed its fees, according to stamp scholar Bruce H. Moshen in an article in *Scott Stamp Monthly*.[1]

According to Moshen, at least 10 different stamps were in circulation at various times. They also served as advertising for the company, in addition to amounting to a bill of sale. Brink's first stamps were issued in 10-cent denominations in 1888. They bear the signature of Arthur Perry Brink and manager W. B. Wyne. Several 25-cent stamps were also issued

and have become scarce collectibles in the 21st century. Moshen speculated that their rarity could be a result of the fact that they were typically pasted on trunks made of wood or stiff paperboard, surfaces from which they would not be easily removable, and thus "became permanently affixed."[2]

Brink's purchased its first motorized delivery truck, made by the Knox Company, in 1904. Sometime between 1904 and 1918, the company issued 10-cent stamps featuring a black-and-white line drawing of the Knox with violet numbering. These stamps have become very rare; by 1998, only one was known to exist.

Brink's self-issued stamp era had ended by 1920 after the company began shifting away from parcel delivery and toward money and valuables transportation. "It seems that Brink's package-express business dwindled significantly as 1920 approached, which might account for the absence of additional stamp issues," Moshen wrote.

In 1930, Brink's sold its package-express business to Marks Express and Teaming Company, and the quaint line drawings of its wagons gradually became collectible nostalgia.[3]

Brink's parcel stamps from the late 1800s and early 1900s have become rare collectibles. *(Photo courtesy of Brink's Museum.)*

a leafy suburb of Chicago, until 1898, when he was offered a general manager position at American Express and moved to New York.[26]

Julius J. Luther and Arthur served as the "active operating heads" of the company, with Luther as superintendent and Arthur as his assistant, according to Seng and Gilmour. They maintained a tight grip on the company's finances, and Brink's prospered under their leadership, rewarding its investors with healthy dividends.[27] After Luther died in 1886, the board of directors paid his son Fred Luther $2,100 to purchase his stock, then resold five shares for $4,200 to United States Express superintendent Alonzo Wygant, reaping a 100 percent profit. Arthur succeeded Luther as superintendent, and Wygant joined the board.[28]

In the mid-1880s, Arthur; his wife, Nina; and their two children, Percy and Olive, settled in the North Side suburb of Ravenswood, an area encompassing 194 acres of farms and woodland that developers had purchased in 1868 and marketed to Chicago's elite.[29] According to the *Encyclopedia of Chicago*, Ravenswood was "designed to be one of Chicago's first and most exclusive communities," though early residents recalled "open ditches and muddy streets alongside the lovely lawns, houses, and trees."[30]

Below: In the mid-1880s, Arthur moved his family into a newly constructed estate at Montrose Avenue and Sheridan Road, an exclusive Chicago address near the lakefront.

Inset top: Nina Meader Brink, Arthur's wife, was a well-known socialite and one of the founders of the Ravenswood Women's Club, which began as a literary club and later evolved into a more civic-minded group.

Inset bottom: Percival "Percy" Brink, Arthur's son, worked as a secretary at the company as a young man. *(Photos courtesy of Brink's Museum.)*

Arthur was well known in the community as a founder of the Ravenswood Public Library, a building that has remained a regional branch of the Chicago Public Library into the 21st century. He was elected a delegate to the 1890 Republican Convention and was a member of a Catholic fraternal organization known as the Knights Templar.[31] Listed in the city's upper-crust Blue Book directory, the family owned several Ravenswood residences and also had a summer home in Frankfort, Michigan.[32] In 1894, they built a lakeside Chicago mansion that was mentioned in the society pages of the day.[33]

"The beautiful home of Mr. A. P. Brink, at the corner of Sheridan Road and Montrose Avenue, was the scene of a most brilliant social gathering Friday afternoon," read one newspaper account of a party attended by 250 guests. "The house was tastefully decorated … in palms, ferns, holly, and mistletoe, and cut flowers. [An orchestra] furnished music behind a bower of palms and ferns."[34]

Union Uprisings

As early as March 1882, Brink's workers had begun unionization efforts through the Chicago City Express Association. An advertisement in the *Chicago Tribune* invited "all expressmen desiring to better their interests" to attend a meeting of the Chicago City Express Association at Brink's Randolph Street office.[35] In the years that followed, Chicago became a hotbed of labor activism. This

HORSE TALES

BRINK'S ACQUIRED ITS FIRST MOTORIZED TRUCK in 1904, but it only gradually replaced its fleet, depending on horses to pull delivery wagons until the 1920s. Brink's purchased its horses "fresh from the range" each year at the Western Avenue Yards for approximately $25 each. The long days of pulling heavy wagons required an animal with endurance and energy. Brink's was "no place for a horse that lacked spirit or could not stand hard punishment," wrote Forrest Crissey.

When Brink's old-timers got together, they would invariably swap horse stories. Before the widespread acceptance of automobiles, the horses used on the money wagons provided Brink's employees with a ready source of amusement, in addition to their transportation duties.[1]

Some horses had such distinct personalities that their names lived on in Brink's lore long after automobiles had replaced them as the preferred mode of travel. One was Charlie, "a huge white animal that habitually traveled with his nose close to the rear platform of a streetcar," according to Crissey. "He pulled so fiercely upon the bit that the arms of his driver could not stand the strain unless he had a streetcar ahead of him to check his pace."

At the time, streetcars reached speeds of eight or nine miles per hour, a fast pace even for a swift horse.[2] In one often-repeated story, Charlie butted up against a streetcar during a payroll delivery to the Cribben, Sexton & Co. stove plant on Erie Street. When the streetcar made a detour into a tunnel under the river, Charlie followed on his own accord. While the horse kept his cool on the ride through the dark corridor, the driver was terrified. Fortunately, neither was hurt, and the payroll made it to the plant safely.[3]

Babe, another horse familiar to those working along Chicago's South Water Street, suffered from stringhalt, a neuromuscular disorder that caused severe jerky spasms in his hind legs. After Babe's original driver switched routes, the new driver embarked on a mission to cure Babe of this affliction. Popular treatments for stringhalt at the time included dietary supplements such as belladonna and potassium bromide, as well as "sweating," a procedure in which the legs were

culminated on May 1, 1886, when 35,000 workers across the city walked away from their jobs in support of an eight-hour workday. Two days later, a strike at the McCormick reaper plant grew violent, and police killed at least two workers. The following day, on Des Plaines Street at Haymarket Square, just a few blocks from Brink's offices, a group of political anarchists gathered in support of the striking workers. The crowd remained peaceful at first, but as it began to disperse, a speaker encouraged the group to "throttle" the law. Police descended on the crowd, and an unknown person threw a bomb, killing an officer. The police then opened fire on the crowd. In the ensuing panic, eight officers died.

During the trial that followed, eight anarchists were convicted and sentenced to death. Every member of the jury had declared prejudice against the defendants before the trial. In the end, four defendants were hanged, one committed suicide in prison, and the governor of Illinois pardoned three.[36] "The trial is now considered one of the worst miscarriages of justice in American history," according to the *Encyclopedia of Chicago*.

Despite the setbacks, by 1892, the city's expressmen had successfully organized. A notice in a March 1892 issue of the *Chicago Tribune* announced that workers from local express companies had met at the Sherman House and voted to unionize. To help increase wages, the expressmen called for doubling the price of trunk delivery from 25 cents to 50 cents, "the latter being the amount allowed by city licenses." A commit-

One of Brink's most memorable horses had a regular route on South Water Street. *(Photo courtesy of Chicago History Museum #DN-0001340.)*

covered with hay wrapped in bandages, then soaked in hot beef brine. "[The driver] took this ambition very seriously and seemed to adopt it as a life work," Crissey wrote. "The experiments which he tried greatly interested the men of South Water Street and particularly the policemen. They suggested one experiment after another and the new driver tried them all. ... Some suggestions were made in all seriousness, but many of them

in jest. As a result, the 'rejuvenation of Babe' became an outstanding classic of South Water Street. The driver declared that 'Babe' did him a very unkind turn by dying just as a complete cure was about to be realized."[4]

Sometimes, the combination of large, feisty horses and crowded city streets spelled disaster. In 1888, a Brink's horse escaped from the company's Randolph Street barn and trotted through the rear door of a neighboring paper store. The horse then "became frightened and broke into a run, dashing through a $175 plate-glass window in the front of the store," stated an article in the *Chicago Tribune*. Bleeding from the cut glass, the horse ran down LaSalle Street knocking down and badly bruising pedestrian Samuel Selzer.[5] Selzer sued Brink's for $20,000 for his injuries.[6] In another publicized incident, a team of Brink's horses charged through a West Side saloon. Although nobody was seriously injured, the company was hit by a slew of spurious personal injury claims related to the episode.[7]

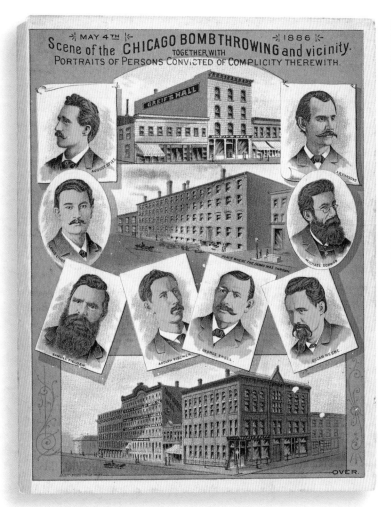

Above: Brink's began payroll deliveries in 1891. Western Electric was its first customer. This illustration from *Moving Money* depicts a typical Brink's payroll delivery wagon, visible in the upper left. *(Lithograph courtesy of* Moving Money.*)*

Left: This souvenir trading card depicts the buildings around Haymarket Square where eight men were convicted of conspiring to throw a bomb into the crowd in a trial widely considered a farce. Four were hanged, one committed suicide, and three were later pardoned. *(Photo courtesy of Chicago History Museum #ICHi-03667.)*

tee was formed to draw up a constitution and bylaws. Nine companies signed the union agreement, including Brink's.[37]

The violent strike by Pullman Palace Car workers on Chicago's South Side in 1894, affected Brink's workers who depended on railroad operations for their livelihood. The national American Railway Union, in support of the strikers, refused to work on any trains that included Pullman cars. Twelve people were killed during the month-long strike, and the railroads racked up $4.7 million in losses. Approximately 100,000 Chicago railroad employees, working for 24 different railroads, lost $1.4 million in wages during the strike.[38]

Payroll Delivery Pays Off

Brink's continued to do well even as the city faced continual social and economic upheaval. By 1886, the company had acquired a freight house for customers who needed storage and for sorting merchandise for shipment to and from the rail express companies.[39] The expansion continued in 1890, when Brink's took out a 99-year lease on a property at 132 West Monroe Street (changed to 711 West Monroe when Chicago began renumbering its streets) at an annual rental of $3,300. The company built a new stable and warehouse on the site for $30,000, and capital stock rose to $75,000.[40]

In 1891, Brink's saw this as an opportunity and began expanding its services, shifting its focus away from solely transporting trunks and parcels to moving large amounts of money. Its first shipment of money, however, was anything but light. According to *Moving Money*, the shipment consisted of six bags of silver dollars, each weighing 61 pounds. It was delivered by Sam Jones, a veteran employee, from Home National Bank at Halsted and Washington streets to the Federal Building downtown.[41]

As the company grew and took on more financial institutions as customers, Brink's directors decided to bond their drivers as of March 1891, charging them 50 cents a month for 10 months, for a total of $5 for a year's worth of insurance. The bond served as a guarantee for the customers that if a shipment was lost, damaged, or stolen, the customer would be reimbursed the full amount.[42] If employees maintained a clean record, at the end of the year, barring any losses on their watch, they were refunded 85 percent of the bond premium.

Brink's landed its first large payroll delivery customer that same year—the Western Electric Company plant, at Kinzie and State streets, which had about 130 employees at the time.[43] The company's reputation grew within Chicago as it built connections with bankers and executives. In 1893, it received the distinction of being selected as the sole authorized deliverer of parcels, express packages, and money on the grounds of the 1893 World's Columbian Exposition, better known as the World's Fair.[44]

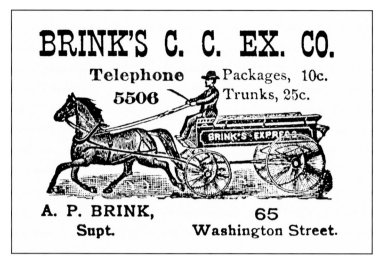

Above: In the 1880s, Brink's issued its first parcel stamps, which were affixed to packages before shipping to prove that customers had paid the set fee. *(Illustration courtesy of Brink's Museum.)*

Below: Brink's began offering moving and storage services in the 1880s. *(Photo courtesy of Brink's Museum.)*

Right: The Transportation Building at the World's Columbian Exposition featured broad, modern curves and a spectacular arched golden door. *(Photo courtesy of Chicago Public Library, Special Collections and Preservation Division, CDA Vol. 5, #70.)*

Below: Brink's served as the official transporter of parcels, express packages, and money during the 1893 World's Columbian Exposition, also known as the World's Fair. One of the company's tasks was to deliver newly minted souvenir half-dollars to the Fair. The world's first Ferris wheel, which rose 264 feet above the Midway, became its iconic image. *(Lithograph by H. D. Nichols, courtesy of The Newberry Public Library.)*

A High-Profile Affair

Commemorating the 400th anniversary of Columbus' arrival in the New World, the fair lasted six months and, according to the *Encyclopedia of Chicago*, was hailed as "a defining moment in Chicago history and the history of the United States as a whole." The Chicago World's Fair proved a wild success, with more than 20 million people attending from all parts of the world.[45]

Perhaps because the teeming crowds made it difficult to move parcels during the day, Brink's made all of its deliveries to the fair at night, "in white wagons which were easily identified," according to *Moving Money*, transporting bags of the Fair's souvenir Columbian half-dollars.[46]

Surviving the Panic

Unfortunately, any optimism the Chicago World's Fair inspired came to a sudden halt that winter at the start of the Panic of 1893, an industrial depression that crippled the nation. The Panic of 1893 was set in motion by bad loans and overexpansion in the railroad industry, as well as a run on financial institutions to exchange bank notes for gold. According to the *Encyclopedia of Chicago*:

[The depression unleashed] destructive forces that shattered Chicago's grandiose expectations of

an unlimited future. … Unemployment and misery savagely struck the city. Tens of thousands of workers lost jobs that winter, as factories and businesses shut down. Some of the unemployed began squatting in the vacant fair buildings and two went up in flames from fires set there, leaving only ruins of what had been a Platonic ideal. The economic woes, combined with the Pullman strike in 1894, was the end of any Victorian excesses. [The depression] seemed to mark the waning of the power of the city's former leaders. Together with the depression, it revealed how ill-equipped the city's institutions were to support the immigrants, industrial workers, and poor.[47]

Brink's, however, weathered the Panic thanks to sound financial planning, even managing to turn a profit while lowering its prices by a dime per parcel and for trunks delivered within the city.[48] The company had wisely diversified, serving not just the railroad customers, but bank and payroll customers as well. Thanks to those wise decisions, Brink's entered the Motor Age of the 1900s with both an abundance of vision and a healthy bank account.

In 1904, Brink's acquired its first motorized delivery vehicle, a Knox Gasoline Express Wagon powered by an innovative air-cooled "porcupine engine," which featured a cylinder covered in 1,750 2-inch steel pegs designed to increase the cooling surface. *(Photo courtesy of Brink's Museum.)*

CHAPTER THREE

ENTERING THE 20TH CENTURY

1900–1918

The lives of working people in plants, offices, small shops, and places of business of every character, as well as those on the streets, are safer because of Brink's.

—Henry Barrett Chamberlin,
head of the first Chicago Crime Commission[1]

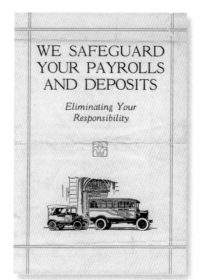

WE SAFEGUARD YOUR PAYROLLS AND DEPOSITS

Eliminating Your Responsibility

IN 41 YEARS, BRINK'S HAD GROWN from a one-man, one-horse express company to a thriving business with 85 carriages and 170 horses. It entered the new century with the capital to expand and update its fleet to serve Chicago, a city that continued to grow exponentially, with a skyrocketing population that rose from 500,000 in 1880 to 1.7 million in 1900.[2]

With more wealth and more people, Chicago was also becoming a criminal's paradise. As Jeffrey S. Adler wrote in *First in Violence, Deepest in Dirt: Homicide in Chicago 1875–1920*:

Tens of thousands of conventioneers, passengers changing trains, vacationers, farmers selling their pigs and wheat in the agricultural markets, salesmen, and others guaranteed an abundance of strangers at any time. This plentitude … helped shape some of the types of locally based crime that thrived in the city.[3]

In the 1900s, Chicago found itself in the midst of large-scale industrialization. Armour & Co. would employ approximately 8,700 workers in its Union Stockyards meatpacking plant by 1910. Telegraph supply company Western Electric, which boasted 5,300 employees at its Chicago plant by

1900, would grow to employ 25,000 by 1917. "Huge factories established regular pay schedules," wrote Alder. "These proved to be a boon for local criminals."

The boldest robbers attacked payroll couriers in broad daylight, helped by "the increasing structure and predictability" of such deliveries. In the aftermath of one such robbery, Chicago Police Inspector John D. Shea criticized police for being gun-shy: "It is about time for the policemen of Chicago to be instructed to shoot to kill when they have a gang of holdup men pointed out to them. [The police] should kill these fellows wherever and whenever they find them committing crimes."[4]

Payroll and Bank Deliveries

Brink's payroll delivery service grew steadily as organized crime became a real threat, and companies became increasingly reluctant to entrust large sums of cash to unarmed employees. Seeing further growth opportunities in the money and

A Brink's sales brochure from the 1920s shows its convoy transportation system. *(Photo courtesy of Brink's Museum.)*

valuables transport side of the business, Brink's further expanded its services to banks.[5]

In 1903, Brink's purchased Schneider's Chicago–Oak Park, a small local express company, for $2,750. The purchase added nine double and three single wagons to its fleet, as well as 12 horses and two mules. A year later, the company bought the small express delivery company of William Daley & Co. in Evanston. These strategic purchases gave Brink's a foothold in two of Chicago's fastest-growing suburbs. In 1892, congestion on Chicago streets prompted the construction of the city's first elevated rail system, known as the "L." The extension of an L-line to Harlem Avenue in Oak Park at the turn of the century contributed to the suburb's expansion from a population of 10,000 in 1900 to 40,000 by 1920.[7] Evanston—home to Northwestern University and wealthy families who had relocated from Chicago after the fire of 1871—was in the midst of a building boom of large apartments thanks to the extension of the rapid-transit system.[6]

In 1904, Brink's landed a contract to deliver the payroll twice monthly to the Corn Exchange National Bank at Adams and LaSalle streets. The $12,000 payroll delivery cost $5 per trip. By 1907, the company had begun delivering the weekly payroll for the Florsheim Shoe Company—the first recorded instance of Brink's not only delivering the payroll but also placing the money in individual pay envelopes and distributing it to workers.[7] Brink's added to its customer list the $10,000 payroll of Joseph T. Ryerson & Son in 1908, and the $7,000 payroll of Colonial Trust & Savings Bank in 1909.[8]

Enter the Automobile

Brink's remained quick to embrace technological advancements. In 1904, the company acquired its first motorized delivery vehicle, a Knox Gasoline Express Wagon. It proved quite an attention-grabber amid Brink's' fleet of 196 horses, 59 double wagons, and 30 single wagons.[9]

1900
Brink's expands its payroll and bank delivery services.

1912
The Brink family cuts ties with the company and starts a new venture in California.

BRINK'S MUSEUM

1918
Frank Allen becomes Brink's president.

BRINK'S MUSEUM

BRINK'S MUSEUM

1904
Brink's adds its first motorized truck to its fleet.

CHICAGO HISTORY MUSEUM #DN-0068759

1917
Two Brink's guards are killed in the Winslow Brothers payroll robbery, a milestone in Chicago's organized crime annals.

on stables and turning barns into garages.[12] Brink's horses had a final moment of glory in 1911 when they took a silver cup in Chicago's annual Work Horse Parade, along with three blue ribbons, four red ribbons, four yellow ribbons, and one gold medal, three silver medals, and 25 bronze medals.[13]

Criminals were also beginning to acquire automobiles. Sociologist John Landesco attributed the rise in the number of robberies to "the emergence of a new factor in our civilization, the automobile, greatly facilitating the chances of escape from apprehension."[14]

Newspapers dubbed the new breed of criminals "auto bandits," Adler noted, adding: "Many robbers arranged to have a motor vehicle and driver waiting to whisk them away from the scene of a holdup."

Such a setup proved especially important in big heists, helping robbers elude swiftly descending police and escape with large sums of cash.[15]

The Knox, however, was not universally well received, especially on the shop floor: "It frightened the horses [and] was cursed by the drivers and hostlers who claimed that its fumes stank up the stables."[10]

On the positive side, the Knox could reach then-unheard-of speeds of 18 miles per hour and had no breakdowns during a test run that lasted almost 12 days straight.[11] Still, horses and wagons would remain the primary mode of transportation for nearly a decade. At first, it proved impractical to replace the entire fleet with a costly machine that remained essentially experimental at the time.

However, by 1910, the motorized fleet was large enough that the company began selling off and not renewing leases

Increasing Violence

By 1910, robberies caused 36 percent of the homicides in Chicago—more than any other source. Between 1875 and 1920, the city's robbery-homicide rate increased 744 percent.[16] Businesses did not turn a blind eye to such numbers. According to Adler, "Anxious to safeguard their money, protect their property, and lower their insurance rates, local

Above: A 1904 Knox similar to Brink's first vehicle is pictured in this vintage photograph. *(Photo courtesy of Brink's Museum.)*

Right: This ad for the Knox Automobile Company depicts a Brink's Chicago City Express truck and includes a glowing testimonial from customer Arthur Perry Brink. *(Illustration courtesy of Brink's Museum.)*

Left: Brink's added its first automobile to its fleet in 1904; however, the company would continue to use horses and wagons primarily for the next decade. This Brink's Chicago City Express Company wagon was in use starting in 1910.

Below: Percy Brink (left) and his wife and daughter are shown here with Arthur and Nina Brink (far right). *(Photos courtesy of Brink's Museum.)*

businessmen added watchmen and guards to their payrolls," ordering them to shoot to kill.

From 1875 to 1889, the few private guards that were employed in Chicago killed a total of three holdup men. Between 1900 and 1920—thanks to both beefed-up security measures and increased robbery rates—48 holdup men were killed by guards.

Police were also alarmed. "I have told my men to shoot to kill," said Chicago Police Chief George Shippey in 1907, in reference to the "cheap murderous thugs who think nothing of killing a man to get his money."[17]

The robberies were not only bloody; they were well planned. Half of robbery murders involved at least three holdup men, who often scoped out their target far in advance of the deed. Chicago Police Operating Director Henry Barrett Chamberlin described them as "heavily armed, highly disciplined bandit gangs who feared neither the light of day nor the appearance of police during their operations."[18]

Evolving Leadership

During this tumultuous time, an era ended at Brink's. Arthur Brink, son of the company's founder and a major shareholder, sold his 14-room lakefront Chicago home for $32,000 in 1910.[19] His son, Percy, a Brink's employee at the time, moved his family to California in 1911, and in 1912 Arthur joined him, resigning from Brink's. The pair then founded Brink's Express Company in Los Angeles, with no records stating any affiliation between it and the Chicago-based company.[20]

According to an article in *Brink's Link*, a company magazine that was founded in the 1980s, the business failed after the economy plateaued. "[Percy] was not a discerning businessman and took several bad contracts," the article noted, paraphrasing Marjorie Brink Royce, Arthur's granddaughter: "The initiative failed."[21]

Percy would briefly work for the Chicago-based Brink's Express in 1927 when it opened in Los Angeles, but soon left to work as a caretaker of

FRANK ALLEN

D R. FRANK ALLEN SERVED AS BRINK'S PRESIDENT from 1918 to 1944. However, according to *Brink's—The Money Movers: The Story of a Century of Service*, he first appeared in the company minutes as the staff veterinarian in 1904, "when he was commended by [Arthur] Brink for the excellent condition of the horses."

In the early 1890s, Allen began a residency at a New York City hospital, but soon switched to veterinary medicine. In March 1889, he earned his doctorate of veterinary medicine from the American Veterinary College in New York.[1]

After his graduation, Allen and his family moved to St. Paul, Minnesota, where he worked for a time as a veterinarian at the farm and racing stable of railroad magnate James J. Hill. He obtained an Illinois veterinarian's license and became the attending veterinarian for several large Chicago stables, including Brink's. He and his wife had seven children and lived in the Back of the Yards neighborhood adjacent to the city's Union Stockyards.[2] His son, John D.

Allen, began working as a Brink's wagon boy in 1904, and another son, Barton, worked as a messenger on the money wagon.

Allen had an aptitude for business as well as animal health, and by 1905 he had invested in five shares of Brink's stock. In 1909, he was named to Brink's board of directors, and a year later he became the company's superintendent of maintenance and equipment.[3] By 1917, Allen became Brink's general manager. That year, his son Barton was one of two Brink's employees killed in an August 28 payroll robbery at the Winslow Brothers plant.[4]

Allen's oldest son, John, who was also a rising star in the company, was named the head of Brink's new banking department in 1917, although he did not always see eye-to-eye with his father.[5]

Allen became Brink's new president in 1918. He presided over the company's national expansion to 49 cities by 1932 and its first public stock offering in 1937.

---

the 90-acre Workman Temple Estate Historic Monument in City of Industry, California.[22] Since that time, no one in the Brink family has had any affiliation with the company Perry founded.[23] Arthur died in 1916 at age 61.[24]

J. H. Bradley, the American Express executive who had served as Brink's president since 1886, became an increasingly absentee leader, coming to Chicago from his New York home only once or twice a year for meetings. Leadership then appeared in the form of another father and son. Frank Allen, a veterinarian who began caring for the company's horses in 1904, had become a shareholder in the

company by 1905. His son John Allen started at Brink's as a wagon boy in 1904, moving up through the ranks over the years. They joined the company's board of directors, and because they lived in Chicago, decision-making was increasingly left in their hands.[25]

Money Specialists

On January 1, 1913, in response to the skyrocketing profits garnered by inter-city rail express companies, the federal government passed a new law authorizing the U.S. Post Office to expand its

Parcel Post service by handling much larger packages.[26] Although the new law cut into the profits of inter-city express companies, the extra competition did not seem to affect Brink's negatively. By that time, Brink's had already begun refocusing its efforts to concentrate on money transport, which had proved much more profitable than the express side of the business.[27]

On March 19, 1917, Brink's separated its money transport operations from its express delivery services, positioning the express side for an eventual sale.[28] Brink's also added breakdown and

consolidation to its list of services that year. As part of the arrangement, armed messengers picked up customers' receipts in envelopes, which were then taken to Brink's counting room. There, the currency was counted, the receipts double-checked, the coins sorted by denomination, and the bank deposits made.[29]

Carefully Orchestrated Plans

Brink's had not experienced a robbery in 26 years when, on August 28, 1917, a band of pay-

THE EVOLUTION OF BRINK'S MOTORIZED FLEET

IN NOVEMBER 1904, BRINK'S ADDED ITS FIRST MOTORized vehicle to its fleet of horse-drawn wagons, although it would be a decade before Brink's began to completely replace its horses with the familiar trucks for which the company is now known.

Brink's First Truck

Brink's purchased its first Knox Gasoline Express Wagon in 1904 for $2,450, an astronomical sum that, at the time, would have bought 25 horses.[1] Coming standard with brass fittings and color choices including carmine and royal purple, the Knox was marketed as "the diamond of the automotive world."[2]

The vehicle's body measured 12 feet long, 6 feet wide, and more than 8 feet high. Its air-cooled, six-horsepower "porcupine engine," considered a design breakthrough, consisted of 1,750 2-inch steel pegs, which enveloped the cylinder and expanded the cooling surface.[3]

Arthur Brink boasted of the money Brink's would save on horse feed,

wagons, harnesses, and horseshoes. "When we put this machine on, we laid off three wagons and 12 horses," Arthur wrote in a letter to the Knox Automobile Company of Springfield, Massachusetts.

Knox later used the glowing testimonial in its advertising efforts. However, the company

---

Below left: This 1904 Knox was found sitting in a New England chicken coop by Jack Hess, who restored it for Brink's in 1997.

Below right: The restored version of Brink's first motorized truck is on display in the Brink's Museum in Chicago. *(Photo courtesy of Brink's Museum.)*

roll robbers held up two Brink's messengers and a driver. Brink's employees, traveling in an open touring car, were making a payroll delivery from a downtown bank to the Winslow Brothers Company, an ornamental iron foundry at Harrison Street and 46ᵗʰ Avenue on the city's West Side. The plant was set back from the street, and at least two robbers hid in the shrubbery in front of the plant.

The Brink's car pulled up on schedule at 10:30 A.M. One guard stayed with the car, while the other two headed to the plant. Brink's messenger Barton Allen, son of longtime employee Frank

Allen, stepped out of the car, and a robber named Edward "Ammunition" Wheed shot him point-blank in the head with a sawed-off shotgun, killing him instantly.[30] According to a *Chicago Tribune* account of the crime, "He crumpled up on the sidewalk." A second shot hit messenger Louis Osenberg "full in the abdomen."[31]

Grabbing the payroll, the robbers jumped into a maroon touring car driven by an accomplice and sped away.[32] According to the *Chicago Tribune*, Brink's driver Kit Lewis, having escaped gunfire "by throwing down his revolver and holding up his

went bankrupt in 1914, and the original Brink's truck has been lost. In 1997, Brink's rescued a 1904 Knox from a chicken coop in Southwick, Massachusetts, "where a disinterested owner was storing the relic to prevent the children in the neighborhood from clambering over the frame," according to *Brink's Link*.[4]

Jack Hess, a retired Massachusetts builder, spent eight years restoring the truck.[5] Hess replaced the engine bearings, cleaned all the parts, and restored the vehicle's woodwork with a type of ash true to the original.[6] "I did everything I could to keep the original intact," he said.[7]

The finished product remains on display in the Brink's Museum in Chicago.[8]

Expanding the Fleet

After the purchase of its first Knox, Brink's also added open touring Model T Fords with canvas tops to its fleet. After the 1917 Winslow Brothers payroll robbery, Brink's instituted a policy of having a convoy car follow behind the money car on each delivery—unless the route included busy city streets where the two cars could get separated, rendering the use of some convoys impractical.[9] The company also introduced refurbished school buses, with armored side panels on the bottom half of the vehicles and thin metal bars running across the top half.[10]

Above left: By the 1920s, Brink's began using trucks with fully armored bodies. The frame and floor, however, were made of wood. *(Photo courtesy of Wisconsin Historical Society #WHi-28402.)*

Above right: Brink's frequently used unmarked trucks until 1927, when it began using the company name as a means to deter robbers. *(Photo courtesy of Brink's Museum.)*

In 1923, Brink's acquired its first fully armored car. The armor was made of fairly lightweight steel, but the floors and frames of these vehicles were made of wood. This proved a vulnerability in 1927 when a gang of bandits in Coverdale, Pennsylvania, used dynamite to blow open the floor of a Brink's truck traveling along a country road on a payroll delivery. The three-ton truck overturned, the crew was knocked out, and the bandits managed to flee with approximately $100,000.[11] Soon afterward, Brink's introduced fully armored vehicles with steel panels as well as steel frames and armored steel floors.

hands at the order of the bandits," called the police, who rushed to the scene.[33]

Police characterized the robbery in newspaper accounts as "one of the most daring crimes of the year." More than a dozen people, including Winslow employees and pedestrians, witnessed the incident.

After a witness in a saloon across the street called in the license plate number, police tracked down the getaway car. Inside, they found a loaded revolver and a torn bag with tools belonging to one of the gunmen. The revolver was registered to Barton Allen, one of the guards killed, and the car belonged to Charles Carrao, a petty criminal with previous arrests for pandering and larceny who also happened to be president of the Chicago Street Cleaners Union.[34]

Police Chief Herman Schuettler called the Brink's robbery a "double tragedy" and a turning point in Chicago crime fighting, vowing at the time that it would "mark the beginning of a new era. It has brought about a police drive against entrenched crime which I hope will not end until every professional criminal in Chicago is brought to book."[35]

After the shooting, Wheed, who was already out on parole for other crimes, took refuge in his mother's cottage on Thomas Street in Chicago's Near West Side. Acting on a tip from a witness who heard the robbers' girlfriends talking in a saloon bathroom, 250 police officers descended on the cottage. "The best marksmen in the department were sent upon the roofs of all the neighboring houses," according to a newspaper account of the standoff. Police bullets "shattered the windows, splintered the doors, dug holes in the brick walls, cut down pieces from the woodwork of the gables [and] made the floor of the small back porch with its little stairway look like a sieve."[36]

A group of 2,000 to 3,000 bystanders stood behind police lines, watching the action. Wheed fired back, sometimes a dozen shots at a time. After a while, a deputy brought in 12 sticks of dynamite and two gallons of formaldehyde, threatening to drive Wheed out with an explosion and toxic fumes. Wheed finally surrendered after police promised not to hang him. "I don't want to be hanged on account of my mother," he told them. "She's old, and she's a good woman and a good mother."

At least 500 shots were fired in the gun battle, which the *Chicago Tribune* called "one of the most thrilling in the city's police history."[37] Wheed and Carrao confessed to murder and named two accomplices in the crime; one of them, Guy Asciutto, worked as a business agent for the barbers' union, and the other, Walter Therein, had fled to Ottawa, Kansas, where he was later apprehended.[38]

Another man, a printing press employee named Charles Benton, was considered "the brains" of the outfit. Factory robberies were his specialty, and he had previously planned crimes for others to execute. A skilled mapmaker, he "scouted through and around the plants he robbed and drew careful diagrams of office interiors and surrounding streets,"

On August 28, 1917, three Brink's workers were robbed of a payroll at gunpoint at the Winslow Brothers Company at 4600 West Harrison, the entrance of which is shown here shortly after the incident. Two men died in the carefully orchestrated daytime holdup. The brazen crime shocked citizens and prompted business leaders to establish the Chicago Crime Commission to crack down on organized crime. *(Photo courtesy of Chicago History Museum #DN-0068759.)*

WANTED: DEAD OR ALIVE

ONE OF THE TWO MEN KILLED IN THE 1917 BRINK'S robbery was Barton Allen, son of Brink's stockholder and future president Frank Allen. As a result of the crime, Brink's swiftly instituted a policy of giving a $500 reward to any employee for killing a bandit in the course of a robbery. This hard-line response was designed to discourage holdup gangs from targeting Brink's vehicles in the first place.[1]

The policy had an effect almost immediately. In 1919, a gang of robbers held up Brink's workers as they were carrying a payroll into the offices of Hart, Schaffner & Marx, a large menswear manufacturing company on 22nd Street in Chicago. This time, the Brink's crew fought back, killing one robber and wounding another. The third escaped "with only a small part of the payroll," according to *Brink's—The Money Movers*.[2]

Brink's approach to crime fighting continued into the 1950s, after a group of masked bandits stole $2.7 million in cash, checks, money orders, and securities in Boston. John D. Allen, Brink's president at the time, said the crime would "never be dead, as far as we're concerned."[3] The crime was finally solved in 1956, just a year before the crime's statute of limitations would have expired.

Brink's used wanted posters, such as this one from 1927, to encourage the arrest and capture of wanted criminals. Paul Jawarski, the man pictured in the poster, was wanted for murder after a Pennsylvania payroll robbery. *(Photo courtesy of Brink's Museum.)*

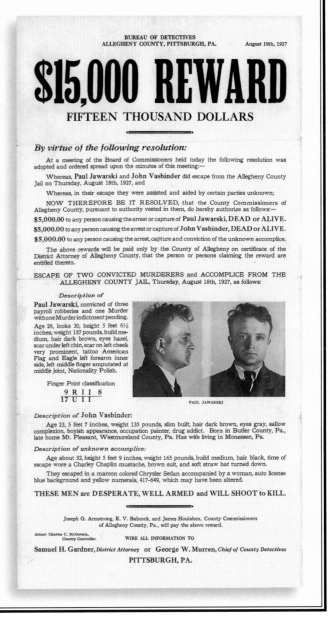

BUREAU OF DETECTIVES
ALLEGHENY COUNTY, PITTSBURGH, PA.   August 19th, 1927

$15,000 REWARD

FIFTEEN THOUSAND DOLLARS

By virtue of the following resolution:

At a meeting of the Board of Commissioners held today the following resolution was adopted and ordered spread upon the minutes of this meeting:—

Whereas, **Paul Jawarski** and **John Vasbinder** did escape from the Allegheny County Jail on Thursday, August 18th, 1927, and

Whereas, in their escape they were assisted and aided by certain parties unknown;

NOW THEREFORE BE IT RESOLVED, that the County Commissioners of Allegheny County, pursuant to authority vested in them, do hereby authorize as follows:—

$5,000.00 to any person causing the arrest or capture of **Paul Jawarski, DEAD or ALIVE.**

$5,000.00 to any person causing the arrest or capture of **John Vasbinder, DEAD or ALIVE.**

$5,000.00 to any person causing the arrest, capture and conviction of the unknown accomplice.

The above rewards will be paid only by the County of Allegheny on certificate of the District Attorney of Allegheny County, that the person or persons claiming the reward are entitled thereto.

ESCAPE OF TWO CONVICTED MURDERERS and ACCOMPLICE FROM THE ALLEGHENY COUNTY JAIL, Thursday, August 18th, 1927, as follows:

Description of

Paul Jawarski, convicted of three payroll robberies and one Murder with one Murder indictment pending. Age 28, looks 30, height 5 feet 6½ inches, weight 167 pounds, build medium, hair dark brown, eyes hazel, scar under left chin, scar on left cheek very prominent, tattoo American Flag and Eagle left forearm inner side, left middle finger amputated at middle joint, Nationality Polish.

Finger Print classification

9 R I I 8
17 U I I

PAUL JAWARSKI

Description of **John Vasbinder:**

Age 23, 5 feet 7 inches, weight 135 pounds, slim built, hair dark brown, eyes gray, sallow complexion, boyish appearance, occupation painter, drug addict. Born in Butler County, Pa., late home Mt. Pleasant, Westmoreland County, Pa. Has wife living in Monessen, Pa.

Description of unknown accomplice:

Age about 32, height 5 feet 9 inches, weight 165 pounds, build medium, hair black, time of escape wore a Charley Chaplin mustache, brown suit, and soft straw hat turned down.

They escaped in a maroon colored Chrysler Sedan accompanied by a woman, auto license blue background and yellow numerals, 417-649, which may have been altered.

THESE MEN are DESPERATE, WELL ARMED and WILL SHOOT to KILL.

Joseph G. Armstrong, E. V. Babcock, and James Houlahen, County Commissioners of Allegheny County, Pa., will pay the above reward.

Attest: Charles C. McGovern, *County Controller.*   WIRE ALL INFORMATION TO

Samuel H. Gardner, *District Attorney* or **George W. Murren,** *Chief of County Detectives*
PITTSBURGH, PA.

according to the *Chicago Tribune*. "He learned when the payroll cars drew up at the door and their license numbers."[39]

Wheed was sentenced to death for his involvement in the Brink's robbery, while the others received prison sentences of up to 10 years. He was hanged in February 1918 along with a man who had murdered a police officer during a separate robbery attempt.[40]

The pair of robbers was the first to hang in the city in three years. The double hanging was intended to send a message to criminals that police and prosecutors were taking a hard line. "The authorities believe this double execution will have a deterrent effect on the murder industry hereabouts," wrote one reporter.[41]

Safer Because of Brink's

Brink's immediately took its own measures to deter robbers and make its operations safer. Brink's President J. H. Bradley promised a $500 reward to any employee for killing a bandit in the course of a robbery.[42] In addition, the company adopted a policy of relentlessly pursuing thieves until they were caught, not only to bring closure to the crime but also to discourage potential bandits from thinking they could get away with robbing a Brink's truck.

Below right: Edward Wheed, shown here in a 1917 newspaper photo, was hanged in 1918 for the murders of two Brink's workers. *(Photo courtesy of Chicago History Museum #DN-0068678. Photographer—Chicago Daily News.)*

Below left: Occasionally, large banks such as Second National invested in their own armored wagons for transporting money and valuables. This particular truck has a side window for bank employees to distribute payrolls on-site to workers at factories. *(Photo courtesy of Brink's Museum.)*

To make its operations safer, Brink's installed plates of ship's armor in the door panels of some of the company's delivery trucks and began bolting small safes to the floorboards behind the drivers' seats.[43] The company also implemented a trailer system for transporting money in which a second car followed the payroll car. The trailer system proved most useful during off-peak traffic hours when there was lower risk of the convoy becoming separated. Regardless of whether or not the trailer system was used, at least four armed guards would accompany every delivery.

The payroll robbery had an effect that extended beyond Brink's. According to Frank J. Loesch, president of the Chicago Crime Commission during the Great Depression, the Brink's payroll robbery was the impetus for city businessmen and alderman to form the Commission:

> *It was a terrible occurrence. But instantly it awakened to decisive action the civic business leaders of the city. They recognized that banditry of the most bloody type had invaded Chicago and that drastic protective steps must at once be taken or Chicago would be at the mercy of murderous bands of outlaws. [The] notoriously brazen [robbery] sparked panic from*

From left, Edwin W. Sims, Samuel P. Thrasher, and Henry Barrett Chamberlin were early leaders of the Chicago Crime Commission, founded in 1919. *(Photo courtesy of Chicago History Museum #DN-0074075.)*

the Chicago Association of Commerce, which issued a desperate plea for taking steps to curb crimes of violence.[44]

The Chicago Crime Commission, founded in 1919, quickly became the leading U.S. crime commission. According to the *Encyclopedia of Chicago*, it "advocated a more efficient, rigorous, criminal justice system that would deter with certain, harsh punishment."[45]

The Commission was responsible for monitoring police, courts, and corrections for leniency and corruption. Steadfastly opposed to plea-bargaining, it pushed for the establishment of the 1930 Public Enemies List. No. 1 on that list was gangster Al Capone, whom the Crime Commission ultimately helped prosecute on tax evasion charges.

Henry Barrett Chamberlin, head of the Chicago Crime Commission when it was founded, also credited Brink's payroll service with reducing crime in Chicago, calling it "a most valuable and important factor. … Its protective benefits … extend beyond those paying for the service to the general public. The lives of working people in plants, offices, small shops, and places of business of every character, as well as those on the streets, are safer because of Brink's."[46]

Behind Brink's armored truck is the Baltimore skyline in 1927. Brink's opened branches across the country throughout the 1920s. *(Photo courtesy of Brink's Museum.)*

CHAPTER FOUR

EXPANDING ACROSS THE NATION

1918–1929

An entirely new development has appeared in America, and especially in Chicago. It consists of the organized use of machine guns by the ordinary criminal classes. … The coarse and common burglar of our boyhood dream is no longer defending himself with a pistol but with a park of artillery.

—G. K. Chesterton, author and historian[1]

BY 1918, BRINK'S CHICAGO CITY Express was a thriving operation with a respected local reputation. However, John D. Allen, son of shareholder Frank Allen and a newly appointed member of the board of directors, had ambitious plans to take the company national.

In May of that year, one of Cleveland's larger banks contacted John about starting a branch in that city. Within two months, John had the Cleveland branch up and running—unbeknownst to his father Frank, who was away visiting family in England, and Brink's President J. H. Bradley, who opposed any further expansion of Brink's.[2] Bradley had been in New York, preoccupied with his duties as vice president of American Express, which, along with Adams Express and Wells Fargo, had just been nationalized into a single wartime entity known as the American Railway Express Company.[3]

Not content with a two-city operation, John avidly began scouting out other possible branch locations. In Rochester, New York, several large clothing manufacturers had "petitioned the company to open a branch office in their city to handle their payrolls," according to *Brink's—The Money Movers: The Story of a Century of Service.*[4]

As John proposed opening a Rochester branch, Bradley, who had already been unhappy with the opening of the Cleveland office, headed to Chicago. Angry that John had made such executive decisions without his consent, Bradley decided to devote his full attention to American Express. In a conference with Brink's officers on March 13, 1919, Bradley resigned and sold his stock to Frank, John, and W. B. Wyne. Bradley's son Ralph also resigned as secretary.[5]

That April, the company's board of directors elected Frank Allen president; Brink's legal advisor, William English, became secretary. In June, John was named the manager of the company's new Banking Department, with offices in the First National Bank Building in Chicago.[6]

In order to buy out Bradley's $25,000 worth of capital stock, John negotiated a large and rather risky loan at Union Trust Bank in Cleveland, where

In 1927, Brink's employees began wearing uniforms consisting of heavy wool jackets with Sam Browne belts, neckties, and metal Brink's badges on their caps. *(Photo courtesy of Brink's Museum.)*

a friend was an executive. The Allens and Wyne "knew that expansion had to come," John told *Finance* magazine in 1954. "[However], my father couldn't help me out financially, and Mr. Wyne couldn't go beyond his own obligations."

In an unusual move, Union Trust accepted the company's future stock as collateral. "I will always believe that transaction gave me the courage to go on," John recalled in *Finance*. "I was always in debt, [always] buying stock in Brink's."[7]

A Move Toward Money

Before Brink's could expand further, there were two formalities to tend to—reincorporation and a name change. To the board's surprise, the 1879 charter for the original Brink's corporation had never actually been filed with the Cook County Recorder of Deeds office.

On May 16, 1919, Brink's reincorporated as Brink's Chicago City Express with $75,000 in capi-

tal stock, divided into 750 shares of $100 each.[8] Eight months later, the company dropped "Chicago City" from its name, as it was no longer solely a local company, becoming simply Brink's Express and focusing almost exclusively on money and valuables transportation.[9]

Brink's main vehicles for secure transport were converted school buses with armored side panels and thick glass windows, usually trailed by a Ford Model T, a ride that Brink's workers ironically nicknamed "the greyhound" because it was more bulky than swift.[10]

Some money transport companies were using trucks with fully armored sides, but at that time Brink's preferred to devote its resources to maintaining larger crews of six or more men with superior firepower.[11]

When Brink's vehicles broke down, these six-man crews also served as mechanics. "There was no such thing as a maintenance department," recalled Vice President of Operations Otto Plank in a 1954

1918
John D. Allen leads Brink's national expansion.

BRINK'S MUSEUM

1925
Brink's introduces its Two-Key Safe.

MOSLER SAFE CO.

1927
Brink's begins announcing itself with logos on its cars and uniforms, in a new strategy to deter robberies.

BRINK'S MUSEUM

BOND BROTHERS PHOTOGRAPHY

1923
Brink's replaces its "school buses" with trucks featuring fully armored bodies.

BRINK'S MUSEUM

1927
The Flathead Gang dynamites a Brink's payroll convoy, prompting many industrywide design changes to armored cars.

article in *Brink's Messenger* magazine. "Every driver, guard, and messenger doubled in brass as a grease monkey."[12]

Eastward Bound

Soon after he took over Brink's presidency, Frank Allen approved the leasing of an office for a proposed Rochester, New York, branch at $60 a month. Rochester was prime ground for expansion, he stated in company minutes, because banks there were not in the business of delivering company payrolls, as they were in some cities.[13]

The Rochester branch officially opened on January 1, 1920, and two weeks later, John Allen proposed a Philadelphia office to the board. He announced that he had received a letter from the Philadelphia Bank Association inquiring as to why Brink's had not yet expanded there, although the possibility had been previously discussed.

John D. Allen responded with a letter stating that Brink's did not want to compete with the banks there, some of which were already in the business of delivering company payrolls. Also, Pennsylvania allowed branch banking, which meant some banks already owned armored trucks for their own needs. The smaller branch banks lacked vaults, requiring the main banks to send armored trucks to collect the currency at the end of each business day for redistribution in the morning.[14]

Fourth Street National Bank wrote back on behalf of the Association, agreeing "not to compete if [Brink's] would commence business there."[15]

In January 1922, Brink's opened its Philadelphia branch and also allocated $10,000 to open a proposed branch in Boston and $15,000 for a future branch in New York City.[16] The money for expansion went toward securing a proper location for vaults and high-security operations, screening and training

Above: Throughout the early 1920s, Brink's utilized Ford Model T convoy cars that followed behind specialized armored school bus–style money trucks.

Right: Brink's early armored cars were unmarked and painted black with gold piping. *(Photos courtesy of Brink's Museum.)*

JOHN D. ALLEN

JOHN D. ALLEN STARTED WORKING AT BRINK'S AS A wagon boy on July 1, 1904. He was 15 or 16 at the time, an eighth-grade dropout earning $5 per week to work the 7 A.M. to 7 P.M. shift six days a week. His father, Frank Allen, also worked for Brink's. Frank served as the stable veterinarian. The family lived in the gritty Back of the Yards neighborhood, which was conveniently located near the Union Stockyards, where Frank had clients.

As was usual at the time, overtime pay and holiday pay was nonexistent for wagon boys. "If you didn't finish your chores until 7, you damn well stayed there until you did," John recalled with characteristic bluntness in a *Finance* magazine article from 1954.

During his delivery-boy days, Allen once picked up the cremated remains of an upstanding Chicago resident and promptly lost them on the way to the undertaker. When he returned to the office without having made the delivery, he earnestly suggested to his boss, Arthur Brink, father of Percy Brink, that they replace the missing ashes with wood ashes.

Instead, Arthur made young John retrace his steps. John recalled searching in every gutter and under every garbage can lid for the missing ashes. This took several days, and John found nothing, but he "never for-got the incident—and the lesson," according to *Finance*.[1]

Despite the mishap, Arthur must have seen potential in the boy, because he promoted him to handy-boy and then platform man, a job that entailed loading and unloading wagons. By the time the Brink family left the business in 1913, John was on his way to becoming a superintendent in the company. His mentor was W. B. Wyne, a longtime Brink's vice president.

Though John wasn't afraid of hard labor, his real talents were entrepreneurial in nature. To make extra money, he engineered a lucrative sideline, working out a contract with Arthur to buy all of Brink's unclaimed merchandise. He would then sell the goods at auction on Sunday, his day off. He also worked out a deal with several churches to pick up their collections on Sundays. He would then hide the collections in an obscure spot in the Brink's warehouse until Monday when the banks opened, and he could deposit the money in the churches' accounts.[2]

It wouldn't be the last time John would work out a deal on the sly. When he was in his late 20s, he was named the supervisor of Brink's new money department. While his father—who was on the board of directors by then—was away visiting family in England, and Brink's president J. H. Bradley was busy with his primary execu-

new employees, and promoting Brink's services to the local community.[17]

The company already had several national accounts, including Kroger and the Great Atlantic & Pacific Tea Company, which eased the expansion, allowing Brink's to enter a new community with several large customers already in place. "Such national accounts have been and still are major factors in the extension of Brink's operations," according to *Brink's—The Money Movers*.[18]

In some markets, Brink's had to educate the business population on the benefits of having an armored car service in its city. As noted in *Brink's—The Money Movers*:

> *Long-established habits had to be changed. A firm accustomed to having its payrolls and bank deposits carried through the streets by a trusted employee had to be convinced that it was exposing that employee to injury or death as well as risking the loss of the cash he carried.*

Brink's also had to prove to business owners that they would save money by using an armored

tive duties as a vice president of American Express, John met privately with bankers and laid the groundwork for Brink's first branch, in Cleveland, Ohio.

Bradley resigned in anger over not being informed of John's new proposed branches, including a Rochester, New York, branch. In response, John took out a rather risky bank loan so he and his father could buy Bradley's $25,000 in shares. The risk paid off, and the company prospered, with 49 branches by 1932.

In 1918, Frank Allen became Brink's president. The father and son team complemented each other well. John was a gifted salesman who understood the need to expand the money-moving side of the business in order to grow. Fiscally conservative and detail-oriented, Frank kept a sharp eye on the company's finances.

Business was going well enough in 1927 that John, in addition to his residence in the exclusive North Shore suburb of Wilmette, was able to buy a 68-acre farm in McHenry County northwest of Chicago, which he built into a country estate.[3]

Tragedy also struck around that time. John's daughter, Barbara, passed away. A memorial to her was built in Chicago's Church of the Atonement Episcopal church.[4]

In 1929, John became president of the Church Club of Chicago, an Episcopal layman's group. He was also a vestryman at the Church of the Holy Comforter in suburban Kenilworth.[5]

Frank ran Brink's until 1944, when he resigned to spend more time with family in his native England. John took over as president, overseeing the expansion of the company's services in 1949 to include lucrative Federal Reserve runs and parking meter collections.

In 1952, as the company continued to grow, John launched Brink's first company-wide magazine, the *Brink's Messenger*. "Discussing the subject with some of the folks here in the Home Office and the branches, it developed that everyone approached seemed to feel that a medium of communication through our far-flung organization would be most desirable," he wrote in the first issue.[6]

John served as Brink's president until 1952, when he became chairman of the board. Four years later, he sold his 44,500 shares of Brink's stock to The Pittston Company and resigned as chair, remaining a director in the company until his death in 1956.

car company for their payrolls instead of handling cash transportation needs in-house.[19] Local police departments also had to support the opening of new Brink's offices, since, at the time, employees were equipped with .45-caliber Thompson submachine guns, which were rarely discharged and used mostly as crime deterrents.[20]

In some cities, police departments provided companies with free payroll escorts. While police departments were usually more than happy to surrender this duty to trained Brink's employees, local merchants often resisted giving up this perk. Brink's

had to persuade city officials that taxpayer money would be better used expanding street patrols than catering to business.[21]

Adjusting to a new city's culture was easier in some places than in others. Brink's acquired Larrimore Armored to establish a branch in Tulsa, Oklahoma. The company's first pickup took place at a two-story office building, recalled Frank Allen. When the guards came up the stairs to make a pickup, the workers told them that was not how they did things. In the past, when the armored car would arrive, the driver would sim-

Left: Brink's Philadelphia branch opened in 1920. This photo of one of the armored trucks in its fleet was likely taken between 1923 and 1927. *(Photo courtesy of Brink's Museum.)*

Below: Kroger, along with several other chain retailers, proved essential to Brink's national expansion. This photo shows a crew making a pickup at a Cincinnati Kroger in 1932. *(Photo courtesy of Brink's Museum.)*

ply yell and the bank deposit would be dropped out of a window.[22]

Brink's Coast to Coast

At a special stockholders' meeting in 1922, Brink's shareholders voted to increase capital stock from $75,000 to $150,000, in three increments

of $25,000 each.[23] The board also decided that year to break off the express side of the business into a corporation separate from the money-moving side, clearing the way for a possible sale.[24]

The increase in capital greased the wheels for further expansion that would lead to new Brink's branches in 49 cities stretching from Portland, Maine, to Los Angeles, California, by 1932.[25] While Brink's experienced many successes as it expanded, New York City proved a particularly challenging market for the company. Many money transportation services already existed, some specializing in high profile jobs such as moving the Federal Reserve Bank of New York's coin and bullion to a new location.[26]

Brink's was able to thrive by focusing on general services such as payroll delivery, cashing payroll checks, and securely transporting the daily receipts from small mom-and-pop businesses as well as some larger retailers. No customer was too humble for Brink's "constantly expanding" clientele, according to *Moving Money*: "Brink's picks up the collection funds of churches and gathers in the proceeds of prize fights, ball games, [and] charity shows."[27]

As Brink's expanded, its armored trucks became increasingly sophisticated and expensive. Brink's side-paneled school buses were replaced with fully armored trucks featuring wooden floors and chassis designed to reduce the trucks' overall weight.[28]

In 1924, Brink's opened branches in cities including Pittsburgh, Pennsylvania; Syracuse, New York; Worcester, Massachusetts; St. Paul, Minnesota; St. Louis, Missouri; and Kansas City, Missouri. By the end of 1924, nine armored-truck companies operated in 16 major U.S. metropolitan areas. Brink's had offices in 14 of those cities and was unchallenged in nine. However, hiring the staff and manufacturing the specialized vehicles needed

in these start-up locales began taking its toll on Brink's, and the board declared a moratorium on new branches until the newest branches in Pittsburgh, Pennsylvania; Providence, Rhode Island; and Worcester, Massachussetts, started to turn a profit.[29]

The moratorium on expansion did not last long. By 1926, Brink's expanded to 19 branches, reached 7,000 customers, and moved $30 million per day in money and securities. A 1926 International Harvester ad boasted that Brink's fleet included 176 of its armored vehicles, 75 of them purchased in the previous six months. According to the ad, "Last year

Above: Brink's employees from the Kansas City, Missouri, branch pose for a picture in 1929.

Right: Before 1927, Brink's crews wore civilian clothes on the job. They carried their guns under their coats. This crew is lined up in front of an unmarked Brink's truck in celebration of the opening of the Worcester, Massachusetts, branch in 1924. *(Photos courtesy of Brink's Museum.)*

the trucks in Brink's formidable fleet, closely followed by expert rifle squads in automobiles, delivered over five million pay envelopes."[30]

In 1927, Brink's purchased a $2.5 million comprehensive risk insurance policy designed, through Joyce & Company, specifically for armored car transport.[31] Joyce & Company's H. Edward Reeves would later become Brink's president. Joyce featured the Hart, Schaffner & Marx payroll robbery in *Chicago Tribune* ads touting its Holdup Insurance:

> *The loss by holdup of Brink's Express Company carrying the Hart, Schaffner & Marx payroll ... was fully insured by the World's Largest Surety Company and paid the same day the loss occurred. We insure you against loss of your money or property by Burglary, Holdup, Messenger Holdup, Check Alteration, and Forgery.*[32]

This truck was used by Brink's Los Angeles branch, which opened in 1927. *(Photo courtesy of Brink's Museum.)*

That year, Brink's opened the wholly owned subsidiary Brink's Express Company of Canada, Ltd., with a branch in Montreal—its first international branch.[33] A Los Angeles branch opened as well, with Percy Brink working for a short time as an agent based there.[34] In Cincinnati, Brink's purchased a competitor, Armored Motor Company, and began operations there.[35]

By that time, Brink's had become such a powerful force in some cities that a group of smaller express companies in Memphis, Detroit, and St. Louis attempted to form a coalition to compete better. They wanted a bigger piece of the chain-retail business, a growing market that Brink's had come to dominate. However, their attempts to pool their resources failed because of a lack of cohesion between competing operations.[36]

Safe of the Century

In 1925, as its retail business grew, Brink's introduced one of its most important innovations to date, the Two-Key Safe. Designed by John W. Robertson, a sales representative for Mosler Safes

who had Brink's as a customer, the one-piece metal safe required two unique keys to open, which has led to the now ubiquitous tradition of "Manager does not have key to safe" signs. The store manager held one key, and the Brink's employee assigned to that store held the other. Store managers would place funds into a signed, sealed envelope bearing the amount and the bank's name, then drop it

through a slit into the safe. Retrieving the money required the presence of both the Brink's worker and the manager, each of whom had to turn their key for the safe to open. The money envelopes would then be transported to the appropriate bank or directly to Brink's for sorting and deposit.[37]

Brink's had an exclusive contract with Mosler for the Two-Key Safes and provided them free of charge to customers as part of their contracts. At one time, Brink's owned 20,000 of these safes, with the largest model weighing 4,645 pounds. The most popular was the Type 5A safe, which weighed 1,600 pounds and featured a liability limit of $5,000.[38]

The Two-Key Safes and armored trucks, combined with the well-armed and highly trained Brink's workforce, had a positive impact on safety. As criminals learned of Brink's countermeasures, word spread that Brink's robberies were too tough to pull off. In one example, fear of a confrontation with Brink's guards helped prevent a planned robbery.

In September 1926, bandits robbed a mail train of $135,000 in payroll money on the South Side of Chicago. In the original plan, the bandits would have instead robbed a Brink's truck that carried a $250,000 payroll every Friday to the Corn Products Refining Company in Argo, Illinois.

Above left: Thieves unsuccessfully tried to break into this Two-Key Safe at a Standard Oil Company station in Cleveland in 1925. *(Photo by Mosler Safe Co.)*

Above right: Brink's utilized armored trucks such as this International Model S to transport money in 1927. *(Photo courtesy of Wisconsin Historical Society #WHi-28584.)*

Right: Gangster Joe Saltis, shown here in 1926, ruled the South Side of Chicago in bootlegging before he was captured by police and implicated in at least 15 murders. Saltis' gang planned to rob a Brink's truck to help pay for his criminal defense, but grew wary of the company's reputation at the last minute and held up a payroll train instead. *(Photo courtesy of Chicago History Museum #DN-0087003. Photographer—Chicago Daily News.)*

THE COVERDALE ROBBERY

BEFORE 1927, ARMORED TRUCKS WERE CON-structed with wooden floors and chas-sis. At the time, manufacturers considered keeping the truck lightweight more important than covering areas out of the shooting range of potential bandits. That industrywide practice changed on March 12, 1927, when nine members of the Flathead Gang robbed a Brink's convoy on its way to deliver a $104,000 payroll to the Pitts-burgh Terminal Coal Company.

Well-versed in the convoy's route and the amount of money it carried, the gang camped out on a remote country road in Coverdale, Penn-sylvania, waiting for the convoy to approach. They yanked out a tree and ran a wire from the resulting pit to the road, "where, for two car

The robbers were to park a hay wagon in the middle of Archer Avenue on Chicago's South Side just as the Brink's armored car approached, and accord-ing to newspaper reports, "when the money guards stepped out to remove it, shoot it out with them."

The money was to go toward the criminal defense of hard-up gangsters Joe Saltis and Frank McErlane, who, before their arrests, "ruled the South Side in the booze, beer, and alcohol busi-ness," according to the *Chicago Tribune*.[39]

"Polack Joe" Saltis had once been a barkeeper, but after Prohibition, he aligned himself with Johnny Torrio, the leader of beer and liquor trafficking in Chicago and Al Capone's mentor. The Illinois Crime Survey of 1929 called McErlane "the most brutal gunman who ever pulled a trigger in Chicago."[40]

However, tough as they were, McErlane and Saltis grew reluctant to face Brink's guards in a direct confrontation.[41]

A tipster informed police of the imminent crime, which was ultimately "sidetracked for the easier one of holding up two mail clerks carrying payroll by train to Harvey, Illinois," which did not involve shooting. According to the *Chicago Tribune*:

lengths, dynamite was planted in tubes or gas pipe," according to *Moving Money*. They also cut the phone wires in the area.

On the day of the robbery, seven armed bandits hid behind the upturned tree and detonated the explosives when the convoy approached.

The intent was to blow up the armored truck through the floor, where it was most vulnerable. The Flathead Gang missed their target slightly, since the truck was traveling faster than the speed they had calculated, but were still able to do enough damage to overturn it and blow it open.

The convoy car was also wrecked in the blast, landing in the crater caused by the explosion. Fortunately, none of the Brink's guards were badly injured, but they were stunned, "and so were unable to resist the armed robbers who instantly surrounded the wreckage," according to *Brink's Messenger*.[1]

Holding the guards at gunpoint, the bandits were able to escape in a nearby getaway car, a blue Stearns-Knight touring model, with $103,834.38. Neighbors had to drive to the nearest town to call police, since the phone wires had been cut prior to the robbery. The delay allowed the gang to escape on a side road to the nearby farmhouse of accomplice Joe Weckoski.[2]

Right away, the media recognized the significance of the event. As reported in an article on the robbery in that day's late edition of the *New York Times*, "Bandits demonstrated today that they had found a way to beat the armored car, which banks and businessmen hitherto have been using successfully to protect large sums of money."[3]

The gang soon dispersed from the farmhouse, leaving their leader, Paul Jawarski, holed up with $37,000. Jawarski, a Polish immigrant and former church choirboy from Detroit, had the "flat head" from which the gang received its nickname. He was captured within 24 hours of the robbery, convicted within a month, and went to jail. He also "squealed on the rest of the gang and gave their identities to police," according to H. Edward Reeves, Brink's legal advisor at the time.[4]

Jawarski managed to escape from jail in a shootout with guards, but was recaptured and sentenced to death for an earlier payroll killing. He ultimately admitted to 26 murders before he died in the electric chair.

The rest of the stolen money was never recovered. A recent *Pittsburgh Magazine* article quoted an elderly resident of Bethel, Pennsylvania, near where the robbery occurred, as saying he remembered when people in the area "searched for coins that might have been overlooked." Others said "hunters around there still look in caves ... for 'armored car money.'"[5]

Almost immediately after the robbery, manufacturers such as International Harvester began redesigning armored cars to include all-steel construction throughout. By 1931, steel was switched out for aluminum for a lighter ride. "That incident ... did more to reveal [the armored car's] structural weaknesses than had nine years of persistent laboratory experimentation," wrote Brink's historian Forrest Crissey.[6]

To commit the Brink's Express robbery would have necessitated a battle with the guards. The train robbery was bloodless. The Brink's Express Company armored car had recently been augmented with a machine gun and, since the tip-off

This 1929 photo shows one of the earliest Brink's armored convoy cars. They were used to transport armed guards, not cargo. Brink's bought armored coupes such as this one as late as 1940. *(Photo courtesy of Brink's Museum.)*

to police, has been closely followed by … sharp-shooters. Police believe [the Brink's robbery] was called off and the train robbery occurred instead.[42]

Brink's Becomes Synonymous with High Security

In March 1927, a group of Detroit-based bandits called the Flathead Gang took advantage of a vulnerability in the armored cars of the time—wooden floors. Hiding out along a remote Pennsylvania road, the bandits attached a load of dynamite to a trip wire and waited for a Brink's convoy scheduled to travel with a payroll delivery. The resulting explosion blew a hole in the truck's floor, allowing the bandits to scoop up the money bags and dash off with more than $100,000.

This seminal incident led the industry to redesign its armored trucks, replacing the wood with a steel floor and chassis. The robbery did more to point out the vehicle's "structural weaknesses than had nine years of persistent laboratory experimentation."[43]

Brink's also began rethinking its public profile after the robbery. The company's fleet, which had previously been unmarked, began to bear the Brink's logo, as it was thought the brand had grown so synonymous with high security that it would actually deter bandits from robbing the vehicles.

After the 1927 Coverdale robbery, Brink's began to advertise its brand on trucks to dissuade would-be robbers. This photo shows a crew loading an International A-3 armor-plated truck outside the Marbro Theater in Chicago. *(Photo courtesy of Wisconsin Historical Society #WHi-25245.)*

Brink's introduced check-cashing services in the late 1920s. *(Photo courtesy of Brink's Museum.)*

According to a display in the Brink's Museum in Chicago, "Up until that time, Brink's believed, like several other express companies, that a low-profile appearance was an added security precaution."[44]

Street clothes were replaced with uniforms, which consisted of a thick wool four-pocket jacket with a Sam Browne belt, slacks or jodhpurs (tight-fitting trousers specially designed for horseback riding), a black necktie or bowtie, and a police-style cap bearing a black metal Brink's badge.[45]

The Money Movers

By the late 1920s, some companies had started paying their employees by check, which ultimately reduced the demand for Brink's cash payroll delivery. Brink's took the new challenges in stride, expanding its services to include check-cashing on-site at factories. Some armored trucks from that era featured built-in pay windows with bars from which clerks would distribute cash to lines of workers.[46]

Brink's also became known as a specialist in handling large money transfers. In 1929, Brink's quietly moved $2.5 billion at a speed of approximately $13.5 million per minute when two Chicago banks consolidated. To prepare, engineers made a detailed plot of the area involved in the move and assigned guards and sharpshooters to precise locations along the route to protect the convoy.

The captain of each guard unit received a blueprint of the map and assigned his men accord-

ingly. Streets were closed at a prearranged time to make way for six money cars, each of which carried $5 million. More than 80 Brink's workers were involved in the move, assisted by two squads of detectives, 20 mounted policemen, 40 policemen on foot, and 80 bank police. Amazingly, the feat was pulled off with little public attention.[47]

By the end of the decade, Brink's had become the biggest name in money-moving. The original express delivery side of the business had shrunk, becoming a much smaller afterthought to Brink's growing money-moving business. Executives decided to narrow their focus, dropping out of the express delivery business altogether.

In November 1930, Brink's sold all capital stock of Chicago City Express Company to Marks Express & Teaming Company, which spun it off into a new outfit called Guardian Delivery Corporation.[48] Officially, Brink's was no longer an express delivery company. It had evolved into a specialized firm devoted solely to transporting money and valuables.

Brink's served as the official money transporter of the 1933 Century of Progress World's Fair Exhibition in Chicago. *(Photo courtesy of Brink's Museum.)*

CHAPTER FIVE

SUCCESS IN ADVERSITY

1929–1949

With a huge volume of the city's business being handled on a cash basis, one of the centers for the movement of currency is the offices of Brink's Express.

—*Chicago Tribune*[1]

CHICAGO WAS HIT ESPECIALLY HARD by the Great Depression, which officially began with the devastating stock market crash on Black Tuesday, October 29, 1929. The city's economic base at the time relied heavily on manufacturing jobs, a sector that suffered precipitous declines as middle-class income dropped, leaving thousands with very little money to purchase durable goods. Between 1927 and 1933, the city's manufacturing workforce decreased by half.[2]

To compound the problem, unemployed people from surrounding areas began pouring into Chicago in the hopes of finding work in the big city. Charity organizations and relief agencies, already overtaxed by the rising tide of financial woes within Chicago, could not meet the extra demand for aid from the newcomers. According to Roger Biles in his book, *Big City Boss in Depression and War*:

> *As the nation's transportation hub, Chicago attracted thousands of transients to its already sizable stable of indigent and unemployed. Throngs of uprooted men and women descended upon the city hoping for work and lodging, but they found only breadlines and cardboard shacks. ... Its residents named it "Hooverville" and its streets "Prosperity Road," "Hard Times Avenue," and "Easy Street."*[3]

At the same time, the city faced insolvency, thanks in part to overblown property taxes and a labyrinthine system of government departments that lacked oversight. A state-ordered tax reassessment left Chicago with no taxes coming in for four years, even as the city continued spending at levels based on its previously assumed tax revenues. The reassessment also lowered property values, and Chicago's tax revenues plummeted far lower than officials had anticipated. At the same time, a group of large property holders, angry that their land was appraised at less than they had paid, contested the property reassessments in court and declared a tax strike until the matter was settled.[4]

As a result of the chaos, the city could not meet its payroll. Things grew so bad that at one point even public school teachers were owed more than eight months in back pay.[5] Out of desperation, many people turned to organized crime.

"When the Depression seized the city, desperate youth, who might have stayed on the straight and narrow in better times, looked to the mafia

---

By the 1930s, Brink's had become the premier money transportation company in the United States. *(Photo courtesy of Brink's Museum.)*

organizations for promise of a better life," wrote Charles J. Masters in *Governor Henry Horner, Chicago Politics, and the Great Depression.* Gangsters, including Al Capone, opened the first soup kitchens in the city, softening some residents' view of the criminal element.[6]

Brink's Helps with Bank Crisis

By late 1930, some economists had begun to grow warily optimistic that the economy would soon begin heading toward recovery. That recovery, however, never materialized. Instead, troubles brewing in the U.S. banking system only further exacerbated the situation. Cash-strapped Americans were increasingly unable to make debt payments, and as a result the financial industry experienced a series of banking panics as unstable institutions failed.[7]

Brink's played an important role in restoring order after the crisis came to a head in Detroit, Michigan. In February 1933, Union Guardian Trust,

a large Detroit bank, teetered on the edge of failing as a result of bad real estate loans made primarily to automobile industry workers. In such a depressed market, many workers lost their jobs or suffered wage cuts. They, in turn, defaulted on their mortgages, and their homes could not be sold in the tumultuous economic climate of the time.

Saddled with bad debt due to the housing downturn, Union Guardian threatened to close down, pay off its depositors, and operate as a trust.[8] The Reconstruction Finance Corporation, a government lending agency, proposed lending the bank $28 million to pay off its depositors, but only on the condition that Henry Ford agree to keep his $7 million in deposits in the bank. Ford refused.[9]

On February 12, with private negotiations failing, the manager of Brink's Detroit branch received a request from the president of First National, another large Detroit bank. The following morning, Brink's was hired to dispatch two armored cars, each equipped with five armed guards, to First National. No further details were given.[10]

1933

Brink's serves as the official money transporter for the Century of Progress World's Fair Exhibition in Chicago.

WISCONSIN HISTORICAL SOCIETY #WHi-28581

1945

Brink's fleet is branded as the "Liberty Fleet" during World War II.

BRINK'S MUSEUM

BRINK'S MUSEUM

1937

Brink's opens its new headquarters in Chicago and offers its first public stock.

BRINK'S MUSEUM

1949

Brink's obtains a blanket contract for Federal Reserve bank runs.

"Most frequently, runs developed at neighbor-hood, suburban, and country banks when check-ing and savings account depositors queued up in panic to withdraw their funds," according to *Brink's—The Money Movers: The Story of a Century of Service.* "On a good many occasions, such runs were broken merely by the appearance of a Brink's armored car bringing additional cash from a larger bank or from the Federal Reserve Bank or branches."[11]

That night, Michigan's governor officially de-clared a four-day bank holiday throughout the state.[12] Suddenly, the request made sense; Brink's had been sent to transport money from First National to banks at risk of failing if frantic investors demanded to withdraw their deposits en masse.

On the first day of Michigan's banking holi-day, "Brink's was the only place in the city where money was handled," according to *The Romance of Moving Money.* "Even the Federal Reserve Bank was closed."[13]

The statewide holiday was extended to eight days. Brink's trucks were sent out daily with cur-rency from the Federal Reserve to the surrounding Michigan cities of Saginaw, Bay City, Flint, and Lansing. Half a million dollars per day was trucked to Saginaw and Bay City alone.[14]

Above: Simply the appearance of Brink's armored trucks was enough to stave off bank runs during the Great Depression. *(Photo courtesy of Wisconsin Historical Society #WHi-28566.)*

Below: Workers line up on payday at a Brink's check-cashing truck in the 1930s. The money was dispersed from a special pay window on the truck's side. *(Photo by Lyle E. Byland.)*

CENTURY OF PROGRESS WORLD'S FAIR

IN 1933, CHICAGO HOSTED THE CENTURY OF PROG-
ress World's Fair Exhibition, held on 427
acres near Lake Michigan, just south of downtown. As it had during the 1893 World's Fair in
Chicago, Brink's served as the exclusive money
transportation company. Trucks were not allowed
on the fair site during regular hours, so every
night Brink's trucks would descend upon the
sprawling fairgrounds to collect the receipts
from the day's concessions.[1]

More than 40 million people attended the
fair, which, as the *Encyclopedia of Chicago* explained, "came to symbolize hope for Chicago's
and America's future" in the midst of the Great
Depression. The focus was on science and industry, with the unofficial motto "Science Finds,
Industry Applies, Man Conforms." Streamlined
and modernistic, the architecture was more akin

A wagon, an armored car, and Two-Key Safes were featured in
Brink's display in the Century of Progress World's Fair Exhibition
in Chicago in 1933. *(Photo by Kaufmann-Fabry.)*

to futuristic Art Deco designs than the ornate,
Greco-Roman style of the 1893 buildings.[2]

In keeping with the themes of industry and
innovation, nearly two dozen corporations had
their own pavilions and displays that, according
to the *Encyclopedia of Chicago*, "insisted that
Americans needed to spend money and mod-
ernize everything from their houses to their
cars." The fair was extended to 1934, partly at
the urging of President Franklin D. Roosevelt,
who considered the fair a good way to encourage
consumer spending.[3]

During this time, Brink's also handled payrolls and held deposits until the as-yet-undetermined date when the banks would reopen. To meet the demand, the company hired 80 additional clerks and rented vacant office space.[15]

The strategy helped Brink's gain more clients, as noted in the *New York Times*:

[Sinclair Oil Company] made arrangements with Brink's Express Company Inc. to transport an additional $250,000 in cash [for its payrolls]. The company has announced that all firms and individuals receiving Sinclair checks will be able to cash them immediately at the express company's office in Detroit. Sinclair also hired Brink's to collect and hold in Brink's vaults all the cash received at Sinclair gas stations in Detroit, Flint, Grand Rapids, Kalamazoo, Jackson, and Battle Creek, Michigan.[16]

Susan Kennedy Estabrook chronicled the Michigan incident in her book *The Banking Crisis of 1933*: "Armored trucks sped currency from New York and Chicago; $40 million arrived by midnight on the 14th. In cooperation, the public utilities commissioner asked for extensions on current bills, and life insurance companies arranged to accept checks as conditional payment of premiums."[17]

The crisis affected 550 banks in Michigan, with $1.5 billion from 900,000 depositors frozen. In what Elmus Wicker, author of *The Banking Panics of the Great Depression*, called "the most exasperating two weeks in 20th century financial history," legislators could not agree on when to reopen Michigan's banks, which led to more uncertainty in

surrounding states. Ohio, Indiana, and Illinois "promptly placed restrictions on deposit withdrawals, [and] repercussions spread rapidly to more than 30 states."[18]

In response, newly inaugurated President Franklin D. Roosevelt held his first fireside chat, declaring a national bank holiday beginning March 6, 1933. When the national holiday began, Brink's

Above: In the 1930s, Brink's introduced all-aluminum armored trucks, which proved faster than older steel trucks and weighed less than previous models. Brink's trucks were advertised as both bulletproof and tear gas–proof, and came equipped with tear gas bombs, gas masks, rifles, revolvers, and machine guns.

Below: Brink's moved into its new headquarters at 711 W. Monroe Street in Chicago, shown here in a sales brochure from 1937. *(Photos courtesy of Brink's Museum.)*

stepped up to fill in for its customers, especially in the Chicago region where it was headquartered. "Many customers, unable to make normal bank deposits, were sending in funds to be held for them in Brink's vaults," according to *Brink's—The Money Movers*. "Hundreds of other businesses, not customers of Brink's, were phoning for help."[19]

To help handle all the traffic, Brink's rented an empty building at LaSalle and Monroe streets in Chicago's financial district and operated as a de facto bank, taking in, paying out, and transferring

---

SAFECRACKERS

WHEN IT CAME TO TWO-KEY SAFES, THE tagline "Only Brink's can open this safe" was no exaggeration. Through the years, industrious thieves tried their best to break into the metal strongboxes, with little success. The attempts only further enhanced Brink's legendary reputation for safety. Because of that reputation, a group of desperate, creative thieves in 1930 realized they had no chance of cracking a Brink's safe at the crime scene.

When they held up the Mulvihill-Goodwine Beverage Company on Chicago's Near West Side, they forced dock employees to load the safe onto the robbery truck, threatening them at gunpoint. They then "drove off after taking two acetylene torches with which to open the safe," according to the *Chicago Tribune*. Even the torches, however, could not penetrate the safe.[1]

This incident may have inspired copycats. Later that year, safecrackers tried to blow up a Brink's safe in the Chicago office of the Ironworkers Union. However, instead of blowing up the safe, the explosives only knocked off part of the lock. Employees elsewhere in the building heard the explosion and notified the bomb squad, which arrived to find the damaged safe still uncompromised, a testament to Brink's focus on security.[2]

---

funds. "Phone lines were run in and the necessary equipment to carry on delivery operations was installed," noted *Brink's—The Money Movers*. "Scores of clerks were hired to sort and count the money and keep the records."[20]

By March 11, according to the *Chicago Tribune*, Brink's moved $50 million in cash each day between the Federal Reserve and banks all across the country:

> With a huge volume of the city's business being handled on a cash basis, one of the centers for the movement of currency is the offices of Brink's Express. In addition to the Chicago movements, the concern is headquarters for a general movement of cash throughout the country which amounts to about $500 million daily. [Trucks] have been operating night and day in keeping the wheels of commerce moving.[21]

Brink's executives split their time between the LaSalle Street operation and Brink's offices at 571 W. Jackson Boulevard. "By the latter part of the week Brink's was handling some 800 daily express shipments of funds in addition to its other duties," according to *Brink's—The Money Movers*. By the end of the week, "the Chicago vaults alone held some 40,000 deposits, with $45 million in cash waiting to go back into the banks when they reopened."[22]

Despite the hard work, Brink's made little or no money on the effort. As explained in *Brink's—The Money Movers*:

> According to a public statement made by Frank Allen at that time, it was not a profit venture, being undertaken primarily as a public service. There were no set rates for these special services. All [clients] paid something. Some concerns voluntarily paid generous sums. If thought excessive, refunds were made by Brink's.[23]

Prospering During the Depression

Despite the faltering economy, Brink's revenue growth continued during the Depression, with the help of new services such as on-site check-cashing at factories and regular Federal Reserve runs.[24] By 1931, the company had grown almost 10 times larger than it had been in 1919.[25] Brink's share-

This group photo shows a typical Brink's crew in the 1930s. *(Photo by Dave Kleiman Studios.)*

holders reaped quite substantial rewards, with ample quarterly dividends from 1931 to 1936.[26] In 1934, its 75th anniversary, the company changed its name from Brink's Express to Brink's, Incorporated.[27]

The company did so well during the Depression that it was able to buy up its competitors in some major cities. In 1934, the company purchased Commerce Armored Car Protection Company in Chicago and Armored Service, Inc., in Cincinnati, Ohio.[28] The following year, Brink's took over Nagle National Protective Agency in Baltimore, and in 1936, Brink's bought Armored Transport, Inc., of Chicago, as well as Chicago Armored Car Company, in 1937.[29]

In May 1937, Brink's offered its stock to the public for the first time. According to *Brink's—The Money Movers*:

> *With the steady growth of the company, the two Allens realized that continued family ownership posed certain hazards, not only to the business but to their own estates, should sickness or accident befall either or both principals.*[30]

The initial offering consisted of 17,000 shares, purchased from the Allens through Washburn and Company.[31] Capital stock was also doubled that year to $250,000, divided into 50,000 shares at $5 per share.[32]

By year's end, the company had assets totaling $2.5 million.[33] To accommodate an increased demand for money handling, Brink's began construction on a new $200,000 headquarters at 711 W. Monroe Street in Chicago.[34] Billed as the "first building in the country erected exclusively for armored car service," the two-story, reinforced-concrete structure was outfitted with a rifle range; guard "nests" with machine guns and a system to release tear gas; automatic doors; and four electronically controlled vaults.[35] Thanks to Brink's success and sound fiscal management, the com-

pany paid off the $125,000 five-year loan it had secured for the project in just two years.[36]

An Evolving Workforce

As Brink's expanded its infrastructure, it also overhauled its workforce. In just 30 years, the emphasis shifted from single men who could work long and erratic hours to family men who were presumably more trustworthy and stable. According to the company's insurance guidelines for managers from that period:

> *Employ no single men unless they live at home. Employ no men who have not lived in your community at least five years. All floaters' applications will be declined. … Employ no men who are mixed up in politics—who are known to frequent pool-rooms, speakeasies, or other similar places [and] men who are having family difficulties.*[37]

Gun-handling expertise also proved crucial for potential new hires, which meant that military veterans often stood out as the most qualified candidates. According to a 1930s employee rule book, a guard "must master completely" his weaponry and "act as if he knew every situation to be dangerous." To keep their skills sharp, some employees competed on revolver teams in their spare time.

Crew members were required to report fellow employees' carelessness on the job, and insurance requirements stipulated that managers perform a background check on all new hires.[38] Prospective employees were charged fees ranging from $2.50 to $7.50 an hour "for the purpose of checking the statements made on the bond application," as protection "against the acts of a dishonest employee."[39]

Weathering Wartime

World War II brought new challenges at Brink's. While the need for services expanded during the war to include payroll services at army bases and war manufacturing plants, U.S. workforce levels plummeted as men and women headed off to war.

"We had a pretty rough time during World War II," said Brink's Vice President Otto Plank in a 1954 article in the *Brink's Messenger*. "Industry was expanding and crying for more and more of our services when it was just about impossible for us to get suitable labor."

Plank recalled that when a small branch in New Bedford, Massachusetts, took on the payroll for 19,000 civilian workers building an army camp,

Brink's "had to draw payroll clerks from several of our New England branches to assist in putting up the payroll, and rounded up police chiefs of practically every town on Cape Cod" to work security.[40]

As the war dragged on and draft restrictions eased, the labor shortage accelerated. "In common with other employers, the manpower shortage is of serious concern to us," Frank Allen stated in Brink's 1943 Annual Report. "Since fathers are now being drafted in large numbers, the situation is becoming acute, and it appears that some curtailment of our operations may become necessary."[41]

Though still not permitted to work as guards, women replaced men in many office jobs during the war, especially in roles processing notes and money. Guards were often spread thin, working overtime to fill positions left vacant. The increase in overtime pay meant profits took a hit, despite a jump in revenue. "To meet the demands for our services, long hours of work have been required of our operating personnel," read the company's 1944 Annual Report. "Therefore wages to a very considerable extent have been paid at overtime rates," resulting

WAR RATIONING

AFTER THE BOMBING OF PEARL HARBOR ON DECEMBER 7, 1941, the U.S. government began rationing tires and retreads, as well as gasoline and many other materials used in the production and maintenance of trucks and cars. The intent was to conserve those materials for use in the war effort. For the next four years, local volunteer boards handled the task of dispersing rationed goods such as tires.[1] For fleet-dependent companies such as Brink's, that ration was often miniscule. A newspaper account from 1942 stated that in October Brink's received a permit for just 16 tires and nine tire tubes to be distributed to the company's entire Chicago fleet.[2]

Brink's lawyer, Eugene Murphy, ultimately took the lead in working out a tire ration exemption for the armored-car industry.[3] Part of that deal involved making room in its administrative offices for the Chicago Office of Price Administration (OPA), a government agency in charge of rationing during World War II.

A *Chicago Tribune* article from 1944 noted that Brink's four-story building at 571 W. Jackson Boulevard included the OPA as a tenant. Millions of gasoline and tire ration coupons and certificates were stored in Brink's vaults, awaiting distribution to 800,000 automobile and truck owners.[4]

Gas rationing proved less of a problem because, since 1930, Brink's had been replacing the biggest gas-guzzling vehicles in its fleet with more fuel-efficient armored coupes.[5] To survive in the face of the strict wartime vehicle production limits, Brink's began building its own truck bodies and allocating more money for repairs instead of purchasing new vehicles.

Above: Large check-cashing trucks, such as this one from 1939, were built to service plants with many employees. *(Photo courtesy of Brink's Museum.)*

Below: This painting by Brink's employee Theodore E. Frazer was done in honor of the company's 90th anniversary in 1949. *(Painting courtesy of Brink's Museum.)*

in a $56,000 decrease in profits for the year, despite a $300,000 increase in revenues.[42]

Brink's equipment was also affected. During the war, the U.S. government issued rations on new tires and vehicles. Brink's lawyer, Eugene Murphy, was able to obtain an exemption from the government to increase the tire ration for armored-car companies, but Brink's had to make do with its pre-war truck fleet.[43] According to the 1941 Annual Report, "Due to the increased demands of operations and in anticipation of our present inability to purchase trucks, costs for truck repairs and rebuilding truck bodies rose company-wide by $141,000 from the previous year."[44]

Brink's President—and Part-Time Farmer

As the war drew to a close, Frank Allen decided to retire to his native England, and his son, John, took over as Brink's president. By this time, John was already a well-known Chicago business and civic leader and a driving force behind *Chicago Banker* magazine, which in 1941 went national and became *Finance* magazine.[45]

An avid horseracing fan, John made headlines as the head of a group of investors that purchased Chicago's Arlington Park Racetrack for $1.6 million. Constructed on 12 former farms in 1927 by a California millionaire, Arlington was billed as "the most beautiful track in America" when it opened.[46] In 1929, Al Capone offered to buy the track for $1.5 million, but it was sold instead to a business group willing to bid $2.5 million to wrest it from Capone.[47]

However, just 10 years later, the track was being run as a nonprofit and was hemorrhaging money. John and his business partners foresaw a possible opportunity and snapped it up for a bargain price. He was named president of the Arlington Park Jockey Club, and Brink's attorney Eugene Murphy, also an investor in the track, was named secretary. "I feel that high-class racing as a business and a sport has a legitimate place and serves a useful purpose in our community," John told the *Chicago Tribune* when the purchase was announced.[48]

After his wife died of a lengthy illness in 1937, John sold the family estate at 1420 Lakeshore Drive, moved a few miles north into the Edgewater Beach Hotel, and purchased a 400-acre country estate in Libertyville, Illinois, which he christened "Allendale." There, he became a gentleman farmer of sorts, joining other Chicago executives who at the time bought up more than 200 farms in the surrounding areas.[49] His neighbors included John Cuneo, a printing executive and the father of the modern dairy farm, and shoe mogul Irving S. Florsheim, chairman of the Florsheim Shoe Company, which at the time had five factories in Chicago, employing a total of 2,500 men and women.[50]

John also served as the head of Cathedral Shelter, an Episcopal-run social service agency, and was the board president of the Episcopal Church Club of Chicago.[51] In 1939, he was appointed to serve on Chicago's school board, but after finding the board ensnared in some ugly political battles, he resigned a month later, stating that "the press of business would make it necessary for him to be away from Chicago a good part of the time," according to a *Chicago Tribune* article.[52]

THE SPITFIRE

URING WORLD WAR II, BRINK'S PRESIDENT Frank Allen, a native of Britain, purchased a single-engine Spitfire fighter aircraft for the war effort and donated it to the Royal Air Force. The ubiquitous World War II plane was distinguished by its slender, elliptical wings, which allowed it to attain faster speeds than other warplanes of the time. Allen proudly kept a photograph of the Spitfire on his desk at Brink's.[1]

Frank also had many vehicles in Brink's fleet spruced up with fresh coats of red, white, and blue paint, and re-christened them as part of the "Liberty Fleet." The eye-catching patriotic vehicles were emblazoned with upbeat black lettering urging citizens to "Buy War Bonds."[2] The vehicles were so memorable that a restored

1948 KB5 designed to replicate the Liberty Fleet truck remains on display at the Brink's Museum in Chicago.

This photo from 1939 in front of Brink's offices showcases the variety of vehicles in the company's fleet. *(Photo courtesy of Brink's Museum.)*

Full-Speed Ahead

John brought a renewed focus on expansion to Brink's after World War II. He opened branches in Rockford, Illinois, and San Francisco, California, in 1945 and 1946 respectively. Eight new branches were established in 1947 and nine in 1948. The company also bought up its competitors in cities such as Buffalo, New York; San Bernardino, California; Baltimore, Maryland; and Philadelphia, Pennsylvania.[53]

Brink's also allocated a large sum to repair its truck fleet, which had depreciated more than expected due to postwar inflation. "Because of shortages in materials during the war years, improvements to and acquisitions of equipment have not been as large as our provision for depreciation," stated John D. Allen in Brink's 1946 Annual Report. "However, in the past year we have again been able to purchase new equipment, and we expect to make other replacements and additions where necessary. This will obviously create quite a strain on our resources."[54]

New state-of-the-art trucks were also needed for Federal Reserve runs. Brink's had been transporting money between the Federal Reserve and banks since 1932, but did not land its first blanket contract until 1949. Brink's Federal Reserve services prospered because the rise of motorized vehicles led to cuts in train services to many cities, resulting in Brink's eventual expansion to more than 100 Federal Reserve runs serving about 1,500 banks.[55]

Brink's made its first parking meter collections in 1949, a service that quickly grew into an important part of the business. Most major cities served by Brink's ultimately signed contracts with the company to handle parking-meter collections—most notably Chicago, where Brink's also counted and packaged the coins.[56]

The 1940s ended quietly, but in January 1950, 11 gunmen in rubber masks held up Brink's Boston branch and made off with $2.7 million in cash, money orders, and securities. It was the largest robbery in U.S. history, and marked the first of many challenges Brink's faced in the decade to come.

Brink's guards transported $100,000 in "loot" for a Pepsodent toothpaste contest in 1950. Contestants were required to finish a two-line jingle that began "All my friends buy Pepsodent ... ." *(Photo courtesy of Brink's Museum.)*

CHAPTER SIX

PROGRESS AND RENEWAL

1950–1959

They came to know Brink's headquarters well enough to draw from memory a map of every inch of every room, even to the disposition of the furniture.

—*The Great Brink's Holdup*[1]

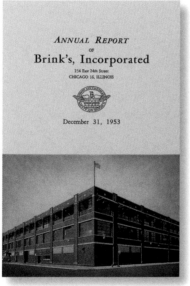

JUST AFTER 7 P.M. ON JANUARY 17, 1950, five Brink's guards were counting money at the Boston branch when they suddenly found themselves surrounded by a gang of men in rubber Halloween masks. The men carried pistols, which they held up to the guards' faces, ordering them to open the door to the counting room and then lie down on the floor. They bound the Brink's guards with rope and taped their mouths shut, then proceeded to load $1,218,211 in cash and $1,557,000 in securities into canvas bags, which they hauled to a getaway truck parked on the other side of a nearby playground.

By the time the first guard managed to free himself and set off a floor alarm, the robbers were long gone, leaving behind nothing but a stray cap, assorted lengths of rope, and some unreadable smudges on the pieces of tape.

The biggest robbery in U.S. history was over in 20 minutes. By the next morning, the *Boston Globe* was already calling the robbery "one of the most perfectly executed crimes of all time," although the details of the heist and the amount of money stolen were as yet unknown.[2]

Brink's executives rushed to the scene from Chicago as soon as they received the news. Brink's vice presidents Otto Plank and H. E. Reeves, alongside General Counsel Eugene Murphy and

Brink's insurance adjuster Walter Palmer, flew straight to Boston to assist in the investigation. Hours after the crime, Palmer was already reassuring customers that his company would cover "a large portion" of the loss.[3]

Brink's President John D. Allen, who had an aversion to air travel, arrived later that day by train. According to the *Boston Globe*, he remarked that instead of capturing the bandits alive, "We'd rather see 'em dead."

He had little mercy for the criminal element: Gunmen had killed his own brother, Barton, during the very first Brink's robbery in 1917.[4] Brink's soon issued a $100,000 reward for information leading to the robbers' arrest.[5]

The names of the Brink's guards were listed in the morning papers, along with their bewildered comments about what had just taken place. The police had little to go on as far as physical descriptions, beyond the fact that all of the robbers were approximately 5 feet 8 inches tall. They wore masks featuring characters such as Captain Marvel,

---

The cover of Brink's 1953 Annual Report showcases the company's new Chicago headquarters in a remodeled building on East 24th Street. *(Photo courtesy of Brink's Museum.)*

identical Navy peacoats, chauffeur's caps, and sound-buffering rubber-soled shoes.[6] They appeared to have taken the back stairs to the money room, where nearly $3 million—mostly in cash—was stacked on counting desks, piled in money bags, and locked in a nearby vault.[7]

On the night of the robbery, the building's watchman was scheduled to have the night off, leaving the guard station unmanned. However, the Brink's guards inside the building were still well armed. Employee Charles Gurell had been carrying a gun in his holster, while the other employees had stashed their pistols on nearby shelves in the counting room. On the wall hung a rack of shotguns. Yet the swiftness and silence of the robbers' approach left the guards unable to react in time to defend themselves.[8] When questioned by the police the next day, they could not even agree on the number of robbers they saw.[9]

Although tips poured in—more than 10,000 all told—none of them resulted in a solid lead for the investigation. Police Superintendent Edward Fallon initially opined that the holdup "was staged by an out-of-town gang of Prohibition-day size and efficiency," according to the *Boston Globe*.[10] His officers began interviewing women who had "been entertained in recent nights in lavish fashion by men known to be tied up with gangs."[11]

Within two days of the robbery, Brink's had tracked down all of its affected customers and sent them reimbursement checks for the stolen money, an especially important gesture considering that some companies feared they might not make their payroll as a result of the robberies. Brink's received more than 100 thank-you letters from customers praising the company for its prompt response.

According to David Kapella, curator of the Brink's Museum, which has an archive of newspaper clippings on the robbery: "This group of petty thieves did a remarkable job of surveillance for months in the wintertime, just checking out

1950

Robbers steal more than $2.7 million in cash and securities from Brink's Boston branch.

T. C. G.

1954

Brink's begins U.S. Mint runs for the Federal Reserve.

PHOTO BY FRANK C. ZAK

BRINK'S MUSEUM

1953

Brink's moves to its new headquarters at East 24th Street in Chicago.

BRINK'S MUSEUM

1959

Brink's officially becomes part of The Pittston Co.

FALSE LEADS

THE MEN WHO ROBBED BRINK'S OF MORE THAN $2.7 million from its Boston branch left behind few clues. In the weeks following the incident, Boston police sometimes went to absurd extremes with their questioning because they had so little to go on. From a public enthralled with the details of the robbery, police officers received an enormous number of leads that turned out to be dead ends.

Early on, the whole city seemed to be out on the streets playing detective. Watchful citizens reported seeing empty money bags alongside roads, psychics offered their help, and train passengers carrying unusually large briefcases were reported as suspects.[1]

Two days after the robbery, a clerk in a Boston novelty store called Daddy & Jack's told police that "a man of medium height and stocky build attempted to purchase six or seven black masks on Saturday. He told her he wanted the masks for a minstrel show," according to an account in the *Boston Post*. The clerk had read the descriptions of the robbers wearing rubber Halloween masks, and thought maybe her customer had been collecting disguises for the crime.[2]

Later that day, police tracked down the man, knocking on the door of his home on Revere Street. He "smilingly told the officers that he had been expecting a visit from them and explained that the masks were purchased for an amateur show given at a Winthrop Beach hall a few nights ago," according to the *Post*. "He felt sure the purchase would arouse suspicions and be traced to him."

Satisfied with the explanation, the police left.[3] That same day, the authorities received another tip: Five suspicious-looking men had boarded a New York Central Mohawk train in Findlay, Ohio, en route to Chicago. When the train reached Gary, Indiana, five detectives climbed on board and rustled the men awake. "Sleepy-eyed, they identified themselves as the National Male Quartet and their accompanist," as reported in the *Boston Traveler*.[4]

The men were again questioned when they reached Chicago, as word that they had been cleared had not yet reached Chicago police. "Again, the five men identified themselves as musicians" and were sent on their way, according to the *Traveler*.

Brink's trucks and the operations, seeing their careless responsibility."[12]

Frustration

The Federal Bureau of Investigation (FBI) soon began its own investigation, since the stolen money included funds from Federal Reserve banks. All told, approximately 3,000 police and FBI officers remained involved in the investigation. More resources were not necessarily better, however. The police resented the federal agents' presence on their turf, and FBI officials did not make much of an effort to work in tandem with local officials. In the weeks after the robbery, the Boston police and the FBI accused each other of withholding information.[13]

Every so often, a promising clue would surface, only to lead nowhere. On February 4, 1950, two small boys from Somerville, Massachusetts, a suburb five miles north of Boston, found a pair of guns at their neighborhood beach. Their father threw the weapons in the trash, but reported the incident to police. A local police officer was able to retrieve one of the guns, which was determined to have been one of the weapons stolen from Brink's guards during the robbery. Unfortunately, by then the trail had grown cold, and the gun told no tales.[14]

The FBI then received a tip that $700,000 was stuffed inside an armchair at the home of the sister of a criminal named Joseph "Specs" O'Keefe. On March 4, 1950, officers also found parts from the getaway truck in a junkyard in Stoughton, Massa-

Left: The winner of the "Live Like a Millionaire" sweepstakes didn't actually win a million dollars—only a week's interest on the million. In this promotional photo, a perky model named Linda Williams poses as the winner, while a Brink's guard stands by making sure she only takes the interest, not the entire $1 million. (Photo courtesy of NBC/Elmer W. Holloway.)

Below: Brink's President John D. Allen chats with a Brink's guard named Erv for the cover of the first issue of the Brink's Messenger. (Photo courtesy of Brink's Museum.)

chusetts.[15] Hoping to gather more information, investigators waited to act on the tip.

Just six months after the robbery, Specs was pulled over in Pennsylvania for a simple speeding violation. State troopers found five guns and another convict, Stanley Gusciora, in the car. The pair were tried for firearms violations and sent to prison, but it would be years before their part in the Brink's robbery would be exposed.

For half a dozen years, nothing came of the FBI's clues. In 1954, a frustrated John D. Allen told *Finance* magazine that the crime "will never be dead, as far as we are concerned. We are like a bulldog—we will never let loose. ... It's a pity the Boston hold-up men were not shot down in the act."[16]

In late 1955, the six-year statute of limitations on the crime would have expired. In response, the Massachusetts assembly passed a bill—aptly named the "Brink's Bill"—increasing the statute for armed robbery to 10 years. According to an issue of *Brink's Messenger* from that time, the act was expressly "designed to help ensure that the bandits who robbed the Boston branch in 1950 will not escape prosecution."[17]

In January 1956, while Specs and Gusciora remained in prison on unrelated weapons charges, investigators finally found a link between the pair and the Boston robbery—Gusciora's brother, who

lived next to the junkyard where parts from the green Ford getaway truck were found.[18]

Under pressure from FBI agents, Specs confessed to the robbery and implicated 10 other men. His confession revealed new details about how the intrepid gang of criminals pulled off the biggest crime in history up to that point. He told the FBI that after Brink's relocated its terminal to Prince Street, the gangsters had watched the operation with binoculars from the rooftops of nearby tenements for two years.[19] Early on, they had identified weaknesses in the security system. Armed with this information, they managed to enter the building at least several times before the robbery and even stole Brink's alarm plans from ADT Security Services.[20]

On January 12, 1956, the FBI informed Brink's executives that the robbery had been solved. John D. Allen felt vindicated:

From the first day of the robbery, we have been confident of two things. First, that no Brink's employees were involved. And second, that the guilty would be apprehended.[21]

H. Edward Reeves, Brink's president at the time, noted that he felt unburdened for another reason: "A worry has always hung over us that the gang, after running out of money, might try it again and perhaps cause injury to some of our employees or members of the public."[22]

Brink's 1955 Annual Report credited the FBI and J. Edgar Hoover's "untiring and persistent efforts" for cracking the case.[23] It did not make any mention of the Boston Police Department.[24]

The Trial

Before the trial, two of the suspects died— one of natural causes likely related to alcoholism, the other from beatings while in prison awaiting trial.[25] The trial of the nine surviving suspects was scheduled to begin in the spring of 1956, but was delayed for several months because of the proliferation of pretrial motions filed on their behalf—1,183 in all.[26] By summer, however, proceedings were under way in the federal courtroom of Judge Felix Forte.[27]

A small percentage of the stolen money— $86,802—was recovered in June 1956 in a metal cooler behind a false wall at a Boston construction company. After a forensic investigation of the bills, authorities determined that the money had probably been stored in sand along the seashore. More turned up when a Boston man raised suspicions after paying with a moldy $10 bill at an amusement arcade in Baltimore, Maryland. According to the *Brink's Messenger*, the arcade's operator "followed the man and pointed him out to police. On his person, the man had $1,032 in similar bills and $3,770 more was found tacked under a carpet in his hotel room."[28]

Unfortunately, more than $1 million of the money, much of it unmarked, was never recovered.[29] The remaining loot, which amounted to

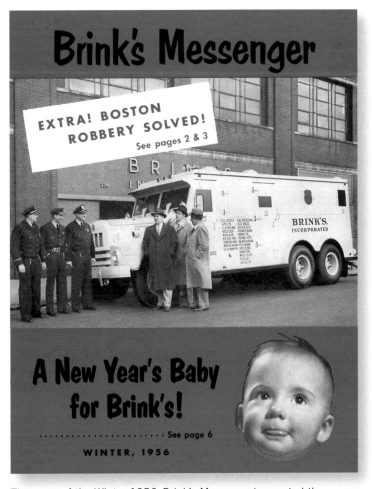

The cover of the Winter 1956 *Brink's Messenger* trumpeted the FBI's arrest of the men who robbed Brink's Boston branch in 1950. *(Photo courtesy of Brink's Museum.)*

approximately $16,000 per year per man from 1950 to 1956, "could have easily been spent gambling at race tracks, in card and dice games," according to *Brink's—The Money Movers: The Story of a Century of Service.*[30]

On October 6, 1956, after 44 days in court, the jury reached a guilty verdict within a few hours. The judge sentenced eight men to life in prison. As the lead informant in the case, Specs received a lighter sentence. Joseph McGinnis, considered the brains of the operation, did not participate in the actual robbery, choosing instead to work in his liquor store that night. However, his reticence did not save him, and he received eight concurrent life sentences.[31] "Not a single person who ever made a

holdup attempt at Brink's is now at large," John D. Allen announced.[32]

Reeves noted that the incident had prompted Brink's to establish a security department and undertake a $1 million security upgrade.[33] Stung by bad press after the robbery, the company also hired Chicago public relations firm Roche, Williams & Cleary, Inc., to advise them on handling future incidents. The resulting in-house pamphlet, "How to Meet the Press," gave managers instructions on what information they could give reporters, and what not to release—customers' names; equipment details; and information on amounts of money, routes, and schedules.[34]

In the pamphlet's introduction, John D. Allen explained the rationale behind the new procedures:

Since what is printed or said about us by reporters goes a long way toward forming the public's opinion of us, you can see that how we meet

the press is mighty important. We don't expect you to act as trained public relations men. But if this pamphlet gives you a better understanding of what reporters expect of us, and how we can satisfy them in the best interest of the company, its purpose will be served.[35]

Released from prison in 1966, Specs assumed a new identity under the FBI witness protection program.[36] Others received parole, and by 1970, 64-year-old Anthony Pino was released from prison, the last of the original gang responsible for the heist of the century. According to the *Newport News* of Rhode Island, Pino's wife told the judge that her husband had "a job waiting as a meat cutter in a market owned by his nephew, and it is the type of work he likes."[37]

Brink's Hits the Highway

As Brink's executives dealt with the aftermath of the robbery in Boston, in Chicago they were

Above: Celebrating the changing of the guard at Brink's, new President H. Edward Reeves (right) shakes hands with John D. Allen.

Right: After the Boston robbery, Brink's issued its managers a set of guidelines for dealing with the press. *(Photos courtesy of Brink's Museum.)*

Brink's underground garage at 711 W. Monroe Street in Chicago featured many modern conveniences. *(Photo courtesy of Brink's Museum.)*

faced with an imminent Northwest Highway expansion that would cut straight through the main garage at 711 W. Monroe Street. They had little choice but to sell the property to the city in 1950 under condemnation proceedings, at a price of $500,000 for the land and $50,000 for damages to the adjacent Brink's office building.[38]

To operate efficiently, they needed a new building suitable for installing adjoining garages, vaults, and offices.[39] After considering several properties, officers settled on a site south of the Loop on Harrison Street between Jefferson and Des Plaines streets.

The company took out a $1 million loan for a new building with the John Hancock Mutual Life Insurance Company, with plans to move only the Chicago branch to the new site initially and keep the general offices in the old building, with provisions for a possible move to the new space later.[40]

To raise capital to help finance the move, in September 1951, stockholders voted to increase capital stock from $250,000 to $1 million. (The last capital stock increase had occurred in 1924.) Stock was upped from 50,000 to 200,000 shares at $5 per share. Shareholders received four additional shares for every one share they already held. An additional $750,000 was shifted from earned surplus to stated capital.[41]

In the end, however, the new building's $1 million price tag proved too daunting for Brink's, historically a fiscally conservative institution. By 1952, the board decided instead to buy an existing building at 234 East 24th Street near the lakefront and sell off its previously purchased Harrison Street site. Remodeling the existing building, John D. Allen and H. Edward Reeves told the stockholders, would save the company a "substantial" amount of money over new construction. Additionally, a remodeled building would be ready sooner than a new one. The general offices would also move to the new site, and the remaining Brink's building at 711 W. Monroe Street was sold to Dow Jones & Co., Inc.[42]

The change in plans paid off. By May 1953, the remodeling was completed at a cost of $675,000. The three-story building consisted of 140,000 square feet on the first two floors for the Chicago branch, and the company's national offices moved into the third floor. Along with an adjacent property for further expansion, Brink's "took title to the complete block" between Prairie and Indiana avenues at 24th Street.[43]

Branches Grow, and So Do Wages

The company had new leadership to go with its new headquarters. In 1952, John D. Allen stepped down from the presidency and became board chairman. Brink's 1952 Annual Report announced:

[John D. Allen] requested to be relieved of some of the president's mounting duties. The company will still have the benefit of his broad experience and knowledge in his new position.[44]

H. Edward Reeves, who had been a member of the board of directors since 1941, was elected Brink's new president. The former president of Chicago insurance firm Joyce & Company, he had deftly engineered Brink's complicated blanket insurance policy 30 years earlier and had been associated with the company ever since. "During this long association, he became thoroughly familiar with the operation of our organization," stated the 1952 Annual Report.[45]

ALTHOUGH THE THEFT OF MORE THAN $2.7 MIL-lion was no laughing matter, there was plenty of comic potential in the story of 11 ne'er-do-wells from Boston's rough-and-tumble North End managing to pull off the biggest robbery in history. As time passed and collective memory faded, Hollywood producers took note.

Billed as "a wild, off-beat, often hilarious comic adventure that recounts one of the most famous and dramatic robberies in American history," a fictionalized version of the Boston robbery hit theaters in the winter of 1978.[1] Called *The Brink's Job*, it was filmed on location in Boston and featured *Columbo* star Peter Falk as ringleader Anthony Pino. Falk studied lock picking and safecracking for the film, insisting on doing all the scenes without a stand-in.

Before filming had even begun, the movie was making headlines. In order to allow the Brink's name to be used in the title, Brink's requested script approval. However, one month before production started, the filmmakers denied Brink's request. In response, Brink's threatened producer Ralph Serpe with legal action a week before cameras were set to roll.[2]

Recognizing that he had no right to use the trademarked name without Brink's permission, Serpe bypassed Brink's President and CEO Hendrik Hartong, Jr., and went straight to the top, cold-calling parent company Pittston's Vice President William H. Sullivan—the owner of the New England Patriots and one of the founders of the American Football League—with an invitation to lunch.

The lunch went well, to say the least. "I have just had a richly rewarding experience, the opportunity to have lunch with Ralph Serpe, who is producing the Brink's [film]," read a letter from Sullivan to Hartong on May 9, 1978. "At the risk of seeming too pontifical, I would like to suggest that my late father, Lord rest him, said that those who poke fun at themselves are people who exhibit a great degree of character, and it is my view that if this is handled in the manner suggested by Ralph ... in the long run, Brink's will be the beneficiary of such treatment."[3]

Sullivan urged Hartong to discontinue any legal action right away so the crew could start filming. "Since time is of the essence, I would like to advise him that this modest request has been approved," Sullivan wrote. "And I would like to further suggest that you direct a letter to him to this effect so that he may proceed without further delay."[4]

Brink's consented, and filming continued as planned. "I decided to use the tactic that I suggest the company laugh at itself," Serpe bragged to the *Los Angeles Times*. "After all, they made a great blunder. Now I'm a great friend of the president of the parent company, who happens to own the [New England] Patriots. I wound up with a season pass!"[5]

The film's promotion proved a publicist's dream come true. One of the scenes featured the robbers frolicking in a mountain of cash after they'd pulled off the crime. Universal Studios hired a Brink's crew to transport and guard the $1 million in "props," watching sternly as the actors "bathed and cavorted in a thick carpet of green-backs, jumping and rolling in the money like kids rolling in a pile of autumn leaves," according to a press release. It took two days for Brink's to recount the $1 million, and not a dollar was missing.

Real-life Brink's guards, including one who had worked at the Boston branch during the time of the robbery, portrayed the payroll guards in the film. Long ago released from prison, three of the actual robbers—Vinnie Losta, Sandy Richardson, and Jazz Maffie—served as unofficial consultants on the production and signed autographs at the film's premiere in Boston.[6]

"Richardson, now a spry 72, still works as a longshoreman on the Boston docks," read a press release announcing the film's premiere. "'The Brink's [vault] looks exactly like I remember it,' he said, referring to the sets. 'They got everything in there just like it was—except for the stash.'"[7]

Brink's Chicago headquarters at 711 W. Monroe Street was torn down in 1950 to make room for an expansion of the Northwest Highway. *(Photo courtesy of Brink's Museum.)*

As the company grew, the directors made a conscious effort to maintain the company's family atmosphere. Reeves' presidency was announced in the inaugural Summer 1952 issue of *Brink's Messenger*, the company's new official magazine. The quarterly's intent, wrote John D. Allen and H. Edward Reeves, was to "bring about a closer relationship between the employees of our 87 branches ... and to better acquaint the stockholders with their company."[46]

Early on, each issue included a letter from the president and a collegial column from John D. Allen called "J. D. Says." In his first column, he related that in "discussing the subject with some of the folks here in the Home Office and the Branches, it developed that everyone approached seemed to feel that a medium of communication through our far-flung organization would be most desirable."[47]

The company continued to add to its long list of branches in the mid-1950s, expanding to cities such as Tulsa, Oklahoma; Lynchburg, Virginia; and Portland, Oregon, Brink's first branch in the Pacific Northwest. Forty armored cars were added to Brink's fleet, at a cost of $6,000 each.

Although revenues increased as the company grew, so did labor costs. Wages rose from 62 percent of costs in 1943 to 71 percent in 1953.[48] When Brink's attempted to reduce wage increases, the Teamsters Union—representing Brink's workers in cities such as New York and Chicago—resisted. In New York, Brink's employees went on strike, alongside employees of other armored car companies in the city. The strike lasted 16 weeks.[49]

In the summer of 1955, Brink's workers in Chicago went on a strike that lasted five weeks. Workers from Brink's smaller competitors did not strike, having reached a compromise. Brink's workers held out for more benefits, but management resisted, since the added cost "would have raised our costs above our competitors," according to John D. Allen.[50]

It was a damaging scenario. Many Brink's customers migrated to rivals that had continued to operate during the strike. "Only a very few of these have returned to us," lamented John D. Allen after the strike ended, and Brink's workers returned to work under the same contract as their counterparts elsewhere.

New Building Designs

After the Boston robbery in 1950, Brink's began moving away from renting existing buildings for its operations and instead began designing and building its own low-slung buildings that emphasized security over architectural aesthetics. In 1956, plainfaced new buildings in Milwaukee, Wisconsin; Hammond, Indiana; and Newark, New Jersey, looked almost identical.

The buildings were deliberately designed with few windows and equipped with bulletproof turrets for armed guards who controlled access to electronic locks on all periphery doors. The building's interior featured armored partitions and heat and vibration detection devices near the vaults to warn the alarm company of possible tampering.[1]

Brink's also lost "several large payroll accounts, which went to paying by check," Reeves said. "Fortunately, this loss has been partly made up by an increase in check-cashing operations."[51] Brink's customers were rapidly switching from cash to check payrolls, and the company could hardly afford to lose their business.[52]

A new coin-counting venture also held promise. In 1954, Brink's partnered with the Johnson Fare Box Co. in a firm called Coin Auditing Systems, Inc. Johnson provided the coin wrapping and counting equipment and cash boxes, which it manufactured, and Brink's staffed the pilot operation in New York.[53]

By 1956, however, the pilot program failed, forcing Brink's to pull out of the partnership and take a $57,500 loss.[54] Reeves unceremoniously stepped down from the presidency that year, remaining on

A Brink's armored car, shown here, makes a delivery at the Federal Reserve Bank of Chicago. (Photo by Frank C. Zak.)

the board of directors. He was replaced by attorney Eugene Murphy, who had previously served as a legal advisor to Brink's since 1934, before moving up to became general counsel, and later, vice president and secretary.[55]

Mint Runs Begin

In 1954, Brink's signed a lucrative contract with the U.S. General Services Administration to transport newly minted coin from U.S. Mints to Federal Reserve banks around the country. In addition, Brink's would also occasionally deliver gold and silver bullion from mints to other locations.[56]

Previously, Railway Express transported most of the nation's coin supplies, with local U.S. Post Office trucks making the final deliveries to area banks. However, with rail transport on the decline, and after several holdups of Post Office trucks, the government reconsidered that approach.[57]

Brink's first mint run, in June 1954, was a shipment of $1 million in coin from Cincinnati to

the Federal Reserve Bank of Cleveland. The largest run at the time consisted of 145,000 pounds of silver shipped from the Denver Mint to western Federal Reserve banks.[58]

The mint runs gave Brink's the boost it needed to make up for declining revenues elsewhere. "Our ability to offer economical rates, as well as furnish door-to-door pickups and deliveries and operate on better schedules, were additional reasons for the expansion of Brink's in these fields," noted a *Brink's Messenger* article.[59]

Federal Reserve banks also required more runs with larger and heavier loads. To meet the need,

Brink's invested in several heavy-duty armored cars, designed especially for heavy hauling across long distances.[60]

At the same time, parking meter collections had become a more important part of Brink's operations. By the mid-1950s, Brink's had contracts to make meter collections from 36,000 meters, including 27,000 in Chicago alone. In 1954, the company began maintaining and repairing meters as well.[61]

Brink's also introduced its Clearing House Service around this time, picking up banks' check clearings and transporting them by armored car to the clearing house—an association of local banks

GOING DIESEL

BRINK'S INTRODUCED DIESEL TRUCKS INTO ITS fleet in the mid-1950s. The company needed larger, more powerful vehicles for its increasingly important Federal Reserve runs, which often involved long distances and large amounts of coin.

The first model in the fleet was a 10-ton armored delivery truck with a tank that could hold 104 gallons of diesel. "Designed for the over-the-road Federal Reserve bank service, she has 'warmed up' in such service between Chicago

and Indianapolis," stated an article in the *Brink's Messenger* in 1956.[1]

Semi-trailer trucks were added to the fleet two years later, for long-distance Federal Reserve runs, and other runs, when available. These trucks had 45-foot-long trailers and could carry approximately 25 tons.[2]

These additions to the fleet came at a considerable price. A semi truck cost $25,000, compared to $7,500 for an armored car. After 1955, Brink's fleet costs rose 10 percent.[3]

Workers at Brink's headquarters in Chicago surprised John D. Allen with an old-fashioned horse-and-wagon ride on his 50th anniversary at Brink's. John started at Brink's as a wagon boy in 1904. *(Photo courtesy of Brink's Museum.)*

Brink's Messenger

AUTUMN, 1954   See Pages 2 and 5

that processed checks and other non-cash transactions and then transferred the funds accordingly. In Chicago, the service involved more than 60 banks, $200 million in clearings, and 76 Brink's workers.[62]

Other new services included toll pickups along the Ohio Turnpike and the Turner Turnpike in Oklahoma, as well as armored-car escorts for employees carrying businesses' bank deposits and payrolls. "For years it has been customary for business institutions in many cities to call on police to provide protection for employees carrying bank deposits or payrolls through the streets," stated an article in the *Brink's Messenger*. "[However, officials in large cities] have balked at detailing police officers for this duty because of the rising cost of police service and shortage of men. As a result, this protection is now being increasingly provided by armored cars."[63]

From Coal Mines to Armored Cars

As Brink's matured, it began formally recognizing employees with long years of service. At 25 years, workers received wristwatches, and every five years thereafter, they were awarded a lapel button. In 1954, Brink's awarded its first 50-year pin to John D. Allen, its longest-serving employee. To commemorate the anniversary, Brink's junior executives planned an elaborate surprise party at the Chicago office. Harking back to John's first day of work at Brink's on July 1, 1904, props included a horse and wagon, derby hats, mustaches, boxes, and cartons.

The company's 1959 centennial was fast approaching. In a way, it marked the beginning of a new era at Brink's. Members of the Allen family still controlled the majority of the stock in the company, but John D. Allen was ready to move on. In 1956, he sold his 22.5 percent interest in Brink's to The Pittston Company, a holding company with controlling interests in Appalachian coal mines and Brink's

competitor U.S. Trucking. He resigned as Brink's chairman but remained on the board of directors. Soon afterward, Pittston announced its intent to buy more outstanding shares, in order to have a controlling interest in Brink's.[64]

Pittston's Past

Pittston's history dated back to 1838, when the Pennsylvania Coal Company was organized in Pittston, Pennsylvania, near Scranton. Besides coal mines in the area, the company operated a 46-mile railroad that was built in 1850. The railroad lacked locomotives—instead, trains were pulled uphill by cable, then coasted downhill to the next incline, instead of in the usual manner, which involved trains traveling through tunnels or going around mountains. Passenger cars were soon added, according to Joseph P. Routh, Pittston's chairman and president in 1956. He jokingly referred to the railroad as the first "scenic roller coaster in operation."[65]

In 1901, Erie Railroad had acquired the Pennsylvania Coal Company. In 1916, the Van Sweringen brothers, Cleveland real estate tycoons, decided to diversify their interests. They purchased Erie and a few other railroads and ran them under the Alleghany Corporation holding company. In 1930, because of antitrust laws limiting railroads' purchase of coal distributors, the Alleghany coal interests broke off into The Pittston Company. The deal included the acquisition of United States Distributing Corporation, which owned U.S. Trucking Company.[66]

Pittston lost money from 1937 until 1944, when it acquired 60 percent of Clinchfield Coal Corporation in Southwest Virginia. Clinchfield's previous owners lacked the capital to mine much coal, leaving Pittston with "great reserves" of the best coal. In four years, its stock went from $30 to $255 per share.[67]

With money to spare, Pittston began looking for new opportunities under the leadership of J. P. Routh. A New York City native with an incongruous interest in farming, Routh graduated from Cornell University's College of Agriculture, paying his way through college by running a boardinghouse and a food-delivery service to the dorms. After World War I, he started a successful wholesale coal company with his brother, then sold his interest to work for Pittston.[68]

Brink's was a good acquisition prospect for Pittston. Although its U.S. Trucking subsidiary remained strong in the general trucking marketplace, there was room for strengthening its armored car division.[69] Other stockholders took the company up on its offer to buy additional shares, but the sale

Below left: Brink's stock was transferred to The Pittston Company in 1959.

Below right: Pittston's Annual Report for 1959 featured photos of Brink's facilities on its cover. *(Photos courtesy of Brink's Museum.)*

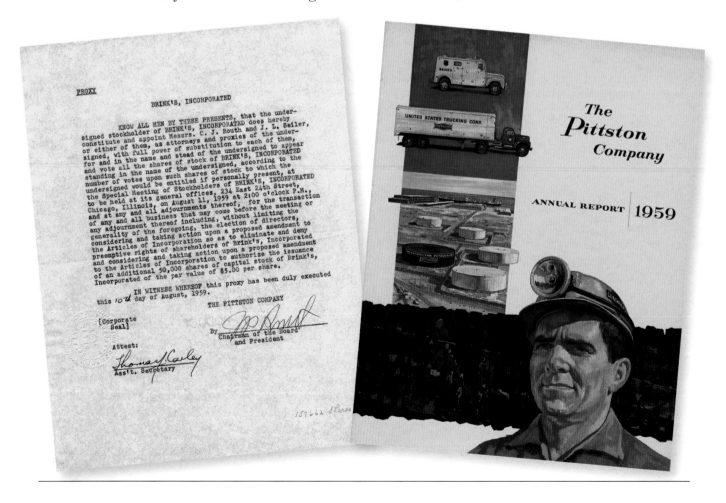

was held up when several Brink's board members opposed the takeover and tried to buy up outstanding shares themselves. After their efforts failed, Pittston sought the Interstate Commerce Commission's (ICC) approval for the merging of competitors Brink's and U.S. Trucking.[70]

In 1958, the ICC approved the merger, but the Department of Justice appealed the decision. Final approval came in April 1959. By then, Pittston owned 80 percent of outstanding shares of Brink's. Eugene Murphy, Brink's president since 1956, moved up to chairman. Arthur S. Genet, an executive from the Greyhound Corporation, replaced him as president.

A month later, on May 5, 1959, Brink's turned 100 years old. A *Brink's Messenger* article about the centennial was short on details of the celebra-

Brink's centennial celebration in Chicago in 1959 included a reenactment of the company's horse-and-buggy days. *(Photo courtesy of Brink's Museum.)*

tion, but did note that Brink's was one of only 57 U.S. firms established in 1859 that was still in business. George Holl, a Brink's vice president who started in 1955 as a guard in San Francisco, noted that at the time of the company's 100th anniversary, "Brink's nationally had 97 cities that they serviced in the United States. ... There were 15 Canadian branches."[71]

As the company celebrated its longevity, it prepared for one of its most exciting evolutions—Brink's leap into the global scene.

Brink's London office in the 1970s was bustling with business. *(Photo by Goodchild Pictorial Photography Ltd.)*

CHAPTER SEVEN

ONWARD, UPWARD, AND ABROAD

1960–1979

*Ours is a brand new world of all-at-once-ness. "Time" has ceased, "space"
has vanished. We now live in a global village.*

—Philosopher Marshall McLuhan[1]

URING THE 1960s AND 1970s, Brink's began to focus on international expansion. Under the leadership of Arthur Genet, Brink's planned to obtain partial ownership in several existing armored transport services across the world, establishing a foothold in foreign countries.

In 1961, the company's first overseas venture came at the request of the French government. Brink's partnered with two subsidiaries of the French shipping firm Compagnie de Navigation Mixte—Fichet Bauche, a safe and alarm manufacturing company, and Via GTI, a public transport company.[2]

In 1965, the National Bank of Israel approached Brink's about establishing an affiliate in Israel to serve the banks there.

"They wanted a serious company that would come to Israel and handle these deliveries of the banks safely," said Yitzhak Rabin, general manager of Brink's Israel.

Brink's agreed to the partnership, forming a joint venture with the three major Israeli banks: Bank Leumi, Bank Hapoalim, and Discount Bank. Brink's retained 70 percent ownership in the company, while each bank maintained 10 percent.[3]

Brink's next major expansion occurred in 1966 in Brazil, where it launched its first Latin American affiliate—Segurança e Transportes de Valores Ltda.[4]

The company found a lucrative market there, and also an especially dangerous one. Roving bands of criminals with automatic weapons targeted armored cars on remote highways that were difficult for police to patrol.

In Latin America, the Brink's crews are highly trained and our equipment is state-of-the-art, said Scott Landry, former vice president for Brink's Latin America. "In this company, the culture of security is very important everywhere," he said.[5]

In 1970, Brink's purchased Servicio Pan Americano de Protección, C.A., a Venezuelan security company with 300 workers, 70 armored cars, and service to 11 cities in Venezuela and Mexico.[6]

The Venezuelan venture ended up losing money for Brink's, partly because of political changes in the country. In 1970, Servicio Pan Americano workers unionized, resulting in an increase in wages and loss in profits substantial enough to be noted in Brink's Annual Report that year.[7]

A year later, Venezuelan banks made an unsuccessful attempt to force Brink's to sell so

This photo of a Brink's employee during target practice was featured in a Brink's sales brochure from 1975. *(Photo courtesy of Brink's Museum.)*

Brink's ventured into England in 1972 with a joint partnership with MAT Transport, a 50-year-old, London-based company that billed itself as Europe's oldest transporter of valuable commodities. The companies operated under the name Brink's-MAT. *(Photo courtesy of Brink's Museum.)*

that they could control the country's armored car services.[8] The tides soon changed for Brink's. In 1972, because of the Andean Pact, which among other regulations restricted foreign companies from owning more than 20 percent of an armored car company, Brink's decided to sell all but 15 percent, keeping the remaining interest until 1997, when it would once again become the majority stockholder.

Brink's entered England next, in February 1972, signing a joint venture agreement with MAT Transport, a 50-year-old London-based company and Europe's oldest transporter of valu-

able commodities.[9] Under the name Brink's-MAT, the partnership also expanded into Belgium and the Netherlands.[10]

1961
Brink's opens its first European subsidiary in France.

BRINK'S MUSEUM

1966
Brink's Latin America opens in Brazil.

BRINK'S MUSEUM

BRINK'S MUSEUM

1962
Brink's launches its Air Courier express service.

PHOTO BY GOODCHILDS LTD. PICTORIAL PHOTOGRAPHY

1972
Brink's-MAT is launched in England.

In 1972, Brink's ventured into Australia, forming Brambles-Brink's Industries with Australian security firm Brambles Industries Limited, a 97-year old business that was one of the top 50 public companies in Australia.[11]

The company's international attentions next turned to Asia, where Hong Kong had become a thriving center for the diamond, jewelry, and commodities market. In 1979, Brink's established its "British Empire" Hong Kong affiliate in partnership with Brink's-MAT.[12] The challenge in Asia was to build name recognition.

"The difference between Asia–Pacific and Europe and America is that in Asia, customers were less accustomed to the Brink's name," recalled Erez Weiss, senior vice president of Brink's Asia Pacific. "They were more familiar with the British companies, and some local companies that grew up mainly on domestic business. ... It was a real challenge to build security, build a reputation, and build the service."[13]

The Sky's the Limit

In the early 1960s, a group of major banks approached Brink's seeking express service for high-priced securities. Registered mail had been too slow for time-sensitive securities that could fluctuate in price during the time it took for delivery.[14]

It proved an ideal time to start such a venture, since the airline industry was also undergoing a change at the time. Propeller aircraft were being replaced by speedier jets, allowing airlines to increase the number of scheduled flights. More flights meant more available space on planes, and airlines had begun searching for profitable ways to fill that space.[15] In 1962, Brink's launched its first Air Courier service after working out an arrangement with Chicago-based United Airlines. Brink's delivery trucks would make late afternoon pickups in either New York or Chicago, transport the cargo to the airport, and then use regularly scheduled airline flights

1977

Five current and former Brink's officers, including Edgar Jones (pictured right), are convicted of bid-rigging.

BRINK'S MUSEUM

1979

Brink's expands into Asia, opening its first Hong Kong affiliate in partnership with MAT Transport.

1979

After selling Brink's stocks throughout the 1970s, The Pittston Company buys them all back. The Interstate Commerce Commission approves of Brink's merger with Pittston.

BRINK'S MUSEUM

1977

After 118 years in Chicago, Brink's moves its headquarters to Darien, Connecticut.

UNUSUAL DELIVERIES

DESPITE ACCOUNTS ASSERTING OTHERWISE IN PRE-vious company histories, Brink's did not actually transport Abraham Lincoln's luggage during the 1860 Republican Convention in Chicago. Lincoln did not attend that convention—he sent his campaign advisors to stump for delegates for him. According to the book *Rally 'Round the Flag*, at the time, it was thought inappropriate for candidates to attend the conventions.

Although it can't claim to have moved Lincoln's overnight bag, many years later Brink's did move the original manuscript of his Gettysburg Address. Brink's has also moved the Declaration of Independence, the Magna Carta, and the Crown of the Andes.[1]

In the 1950s, Brink's established a company-wide policy regarding high-profile hauls: "In general, Brink's agrees to cooperate only when the object has a reasonably high intrinsic or historical value, and when it's to be paid for at an agreed rate and handled in a business-like fashion without horseplay."

Brink's has turned down requests to transport plaster casts of a starlet's legs, a truckload of play money, and, in the 1970s, nuclear waste (a request from the U.S. Atomic Energy Commission). Brink's did, however, agree to transport 1,209,467 silver dollars—36 tons in all—from the U.S. Treasury in Washington to a supermarket convention in Cleveland, Ohio, in April 1955.

"The huge hoard of silver was spread on the floor of the booth of the Gold Seal Company, makers of Glass Wax," according to *Brink's—The Money Movers: The Story of a Century of Service.* Brink's guards who watched over the coins "reported that the silver would 'flow' through the night, giving off a faint but almost constant jingle."

The brand-new, as-yet-unhandled coins also shed silver dust: "When re-bagging them at the end of the exhibition, this dust rose in a silver haze about four feet in the air. It caused a sickeningly sweet taste and finally became so bad that the Brink's men were forced to mask their noses and mouths with handkerchiefs."

After the show, the Treasury did a recount, and found only 17 coins missing, "although thousands of people had handled and even walked over the money."[2]

to deliver the cargo to the other city the following morning.[16]

The first Air Courier shipment involved transporting securities from Chicago's First National Bank to Chase Manhattan Bank in New York.[17] By 1964, Air Courier had established links between 13 cities. Early customers consisted mostly of banks and brokerage firms shipping securities. Gradually, customers also began shipping precious metals and other valuables such as jewels and furs.[18] In most cases, shipments were picked up by armored car in the afternoon and delivered the following morning.[19]

Air Courier had its own set of protocols for guarding shipments. After picking up a shipment, Brink's armored cars headed to the airport and were given clearance to drive directly onto the runway.

An Air Courier guard met the car as it pulled up to the plane. After the shipment was unloaded from the truck, it would be the last piece of cargo loaded into the aircraft's cargo area. The courier would personally observe the shipment being loaded on the plane and the crew locking the cargo door, and then board the plane as the last passenger.

At the final destination, an armored crew would stand by until the plane taxied down the runway.[20] Once the plane arrived at the airport, the courier was the first passenger to disembark, delivering the shipment to a waiting armored car and crew beside the plane. The cargo was then unloaded, immediately logged in, and placed into the armored car for delivery. If for some reason the plane was rerouted, the airline contacted Brink's, and Brink's

In 1969, after the NASA Apollo 11 mission that put the first man on the moon, Brink's distributed moon rocks, chips, and dust to about 60 scientists around the world. The samples—18 pounds in all, distributed to 142 scientists—were used for analysis in university, industrial, and government laboratories.[3]

In 2001, Brink's transported $240 million worth of gold and silver ingots recovered from the ruins of the World Trade Center after the September 11, 2001, terrorist attacks. The Bank of Nova Scotia had stored the ingots in a bombproof vault in the basement of 4 World Trade Center, which was crushed by the collapse of the Twin Towers.[4]

Brink's has also moved hockey's Stanley Cup; tennis' Davis Cup; gold, silver, and bronze used to make the medals for the 2002 Olympics in Salt Lake City; the National Basketball League trophy; and Super Bowl championship rings.[5]

In 2008, Brink's moved fast-food restaurant KFC's Secret Recipe—a tattered, handwritten note from company founder Colonel Harland Sanders. The recipe, which only two company executives have access to at any one time, had been kept in a Louisville, Kentucky, vault behind several locked doors. A firm hired to improve security at the KFC headquarters, however, thought the provisions inadequate. KFC president Roger Eaton did not want to be known as "the man who lost the recipe," so it was moved to an undisclosed higher-security location. A gauntlet of police-car escorts with lights blazing and whirring sirens accompanied the Brink's truck.[6]

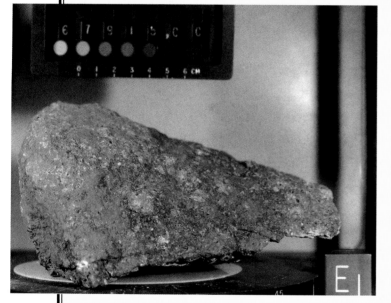

Brink's transported moon rocks from NASA's Apollo 11 mission to universities and laboratories around the world. *(Photo courtesy of NASA.)*

made arrangements for pickup in the destination city.[21]

By 1970, Air Courier was thriving, producing 10 percent of the volume and 15 percent of the profit of Brink's, Incorporated. That year, Air Courier served 135 cities. Each night, on average, Brink's had 28 air couriers in the skies, collectively handling about $100 million of valuables per night out of New York City alone.[22]

Also that year, Air Courier handled 80 percent of the furs "shipped through New York City airports to the garment district," according to a *Chicago Tribune* article. It also negotiated with the Air Cargo Association to ship artwork and industrial diamonds and began working on establishing airport security depots "so that Brink's employees would actually do the unloading of planes and take care of the interim storage of valuable items," as noted in a *Chicago Tribune* article.[23]

The success of Air Courier soon attracted the attention of airlines. In 1971, Brink's scored a lucrative contract from Air Cargo Inc.—a company jointly owned by 33 airlines—to provide ground transport for valuable cargo to and from airports in 81 metropolitan areas.[24]

The venture went so well that Brink's and Pittston executives began actively seeking new ways to profit from the Brink's brand. "The firm continues to look at other ways to expand … and eventually may go into the home security device market," predicted the *Chicago Tribune*.[25]

Longtime Brink's employee Leo Facenda said the company's stellar reputation prompted him to make the switch from working at a financial institution to a sales job at Brink's in 1974. "I guess what drew me to Brink's was the fact that even when I was in the banking world, I mean, the word *Brink's* itself meant trust, meant integrity," said Facenda, who retired from Brink's as a relationship manager in June 2008.[26]

Hijackers and a Hero

The success of Air Courier also attracted criminals. In 1967, a flight carrying $2.2 million in securities was preparing to take off from Chicago's O'Hare Airport when an airport catering truck pulled up. Two men got out of the truck, opened the cargo hatch, took a bag out, and closed the hatch seconds before the jet began taxiing down the runway. They then escaped on foot, leaping down an embankment, where they were arrested. A police

Above: Brink's Air Courier clerks sort the day's express mail.

Left: Air Courier shipments were always closely guarded until they were safely locked in the cargo hold. *(Photos courtesy of Brink's Museum.)*

detective sitting in a nearby car had witnessed the incident and called for backup.

The pilot realized something was amiss when the "open hatch" light on the aircraft's dashboard went on, but at that point it was too late to abort the flight. A half-hour later, the plane returned to O'Hare.[27]

A more frightening incident occurred in 1970, when an armed man on a 707 jet from O'Hare handed the flight attendant a note saying he wanted to go to North Korea. The pilot passed the note to passenger Robert DeNisco, a Brink's air courier armed with a .38 caliber pistol.

When the plane landed in San Francisco, the hijacker allowed 35 passengers to leave, while the rest were told to move to the back of the plane. DeNisco then jumped into an aisle, shouted "Police!" and shot the hijacker in the abdomen, critically wounding him.

DeNisco, who received much media attention for his heroics that day, told reporters, "All I want to do now is pay my bills and get some sleep."[28]

"I Just Got the Blues, Judge"

A "family man" from leafy Oak Park, Illinois, Arthur H. Page, had worked for Brink's for 11 years in 1963, when he decided to remove $71,000 from several money bags.

To avoid immediate detection, Page refastened the bag's lead seals by "pounding them with the butt of his revolver," according to the *Chicago Tribune*. He then put a down payment on a flashy red Buick and drove it to Phoenix, where he went on a three-month bender, wearing $200 silk suits, renting a swanky apartment, and buying a Cadillac for a new girlfriend.[29]

During that time, he practically went out of his way to get caught by authorities. "He had dinner with high-ranking Phoenix police officials, always gave his own name and home address, and intentionally kept [in plain sight] his bright red and white sports car, which was prominently mentioned in 'wanted' bulletins," wrote *Chicago Tribune* reporter Robert Wiedrich. One time, he

even reported his car missing, and rather than nabbing him, police located the car and kindly brought it back to him.[30]

Finally, the FBI caught Page in Phoenix and brought him back to Chicago for trial. He pled guilty and received a light three-year prison sentence, of which he only had to serve six months, having been judged "immature" in a psychiatric report. He also had to pay Brink's back the $19,000 he had spent in three-months' time.[31]

"It was a goofy escapade, but I enjoyed it," he told reporters after his capture, adding that he knew the cops would catch up with him, "if [he] kept driving the Buick."[32]

Driver William Johnson would also go down in Brink's annals as a good employee suddenly gone bad. Johnson had worked for Brink's for 26 years by 1960, when he walked off with $30,000 of the cash he was supposed to be watching as his crew picked up a collection at a currency exchange.[33] Johnson put the money in his pocket, locked the truck, and headed to his favorite tavern, stopping along the way to buy some clothing and a pouch for the cash.[34] He left his Brink's cap, jacket, belt, holster, gun, and badge on the front seat of the truck, along with a note saying, "I'm going out on a good drunk to forget things. This mess has got me insane. I'm ready to kill myself."

The police found Johnson at the tavern with the money in a blue zippered bag on the barstool beside him. "I'm a good guy," he told them. "I only spent $60."[35]

In court, when asked why he took the money, Johnson replied, "I just got the blues, judge." He received probation and was told to get psychiatric care.[36]

Parking Meter Expiration

Brink's had a good relationship with the City of Chicago throughout the 1960s, earning a tidy sum for collecting the proceeds from its 35,000

Brink's offered a $5,000 reward for information leading to the arrest of Arthur H. Page. He was arrested in Phoenix, Arizona, three months after he walked off the job with $71,000 from Brink's money bags. *(Photo courtesy of Brink's Museum.)*

Above: This undated photo was probably taken in front of Brink's Chicago headquarters. John D. Allen, Jr., son of longtime Brink's chairman John D. Allen, is second from left. Charles Allen, a company vice president and son of Frank Allen, is third from left, and Otto D. Plank, longtime vice president of operations, is second from right. *(Photo by International Harvester Company.)*

Below: From the 1950s to the 1970s, Brink's guards marched with police officers in Chicago's annual St. Jude's Day parade. They would then attend mass at St. Peter's Church on Madison Street and have brunch at the Hilton Hotel. *(Photo courtesy of Brink's Museum.)*

parking meters and fare receipts for the Chicago Transit Authority at the City's train depots.[37] In 1968, Brink's even agreed to lend its armored cars to Chicago police for emergency use.[38]

The relationship soured in 1972, however, after the City accused Brink's of erasing and altering weekly coin count sheets, costing the City up to $27,000 in lost parking meter revenue. The City's meter maintenance company also accused Brink's of not emptying meters on schedule, leading to 67,000 coin jams and broken meters in 1971.[39]

Brink's subsequently lost the contract to Jerome J. Robinson's Parking Meter Service Co., a company that had been formed the day before bids went out to the city and underbid Brink's by $700,000.[40] The deal raised suspicion—Jerome Robinson had previously been convicted in New York of perjury in a case involving the bribery of public officials—and Brink's received the meter-collection contract again the following year.[41]

The parking meter flurry proved relatively minor, however, compared to the impending storm of accusations Brink's would soon face. In 1977, Brink's was investigated by the U.S. Justice Department, and five of its officers were convicted of antitrust violations in a bid-rigging scheme.

From early 1968 to 1975, according to the federal indictment, Brink's and competitor Wells Fargo conspired to set prices and divide up territories between themselves so they would not compete against each other. The conspiracy kept prices "artificially high" and prevented competition from flourishing, according to a *Wall Street Journal* article.[42]

Brink's Chairman Edgar A. Jones, Executive Vice President John W. Jones, and Vice President Melvin Rognerud pleaded no contest to charges of conspiring to fix prices. Edgar Jones received a $10,000 fine and a one-year suspended sentence, while John Jones and Rognerud were each fined $10,000 and ordered to serve two months of a six-month jail sentence.[43]

Brink's was also hit by civil lawsuits for the violations, including a Connecticut class-action lawsuit on behalf of customers who had to pay rigged prices for armored-car services. In 1977, Brink's paid $623,000 in criminal fines and $5.9 million to settle some of the lawsuits.

The settlement came at a particularly bad time. "The drastic decline in our 1977 profits was primarily due to an extraordinary charge of approximately $6 million for antitrust litigation," wrote Brink's President Hendrik J. Hartong, Jr., in the company's 1977 Annual Report. "Moreover, unfavorable market conditions in our domestic armored

Brink's guards participated in a promotion with cast members of the 1965 film *The Sound of Music. (Photo courtesy of Brink's Museum.)*

So Long, Chicago

BRINK'S WAS A 118-YEAR-OLD CHICAGO INSTITUtion in 1977, when it announced it was moving its headquarters to Darien, Connecticut. The company had a new president, Hendrik Hartong, Jr., and began cleaning house after five of its top officers were convicted of bid-rigging, which resulted in approximately $6 million in fines. In addition to Hartong, four new directors joined Brink's that year.

The move required relocating 26 out of 70 administrative staff positions to Darien in 1977 at a cost of $1.3 million.[1] The move put Brink's an hour's train ride away from its parent company, Pittston, based in New York. Hartong also already had a connection to Darien—he owned a country estate in nearby Greenwich, Connecticut.

The Netherlands-born Hartong, known to his colleagues as "Henk," was a mere 38 years old when he took over the Brink's presidency. The son of the chairman of Philips Electronics, he had been a Philips group vice president and the former chairman, as well as the president and CEO of New Hampshire–based Simplex Wire and Cable, a 110-year–old firm specializing in the manufacture of undersea cable that merged with Tyco, Inc., in 1974.

Hartong had no experience in the armored car industry when he took the helm at Brink's— he instead represented a "growing trend among American businesses [of] recruiting top executives based on demonstrated managerial skills rather than experience with a particular industry."[2]

car business coupled with higher wage and benefit increases further depressed our operating performance."[44]

Three years later, the company paid an additional $2.7 million settlement to 12 Federal Reserve banks that it had overcharged.[45]

Union Tensions

At the same time, union demands cut even further into profit margins. With non-union shops able to pay lower wages, Brink's struggled to remain competitive.

In 1965, Brink's and unionized competitor Armored Express Company narrowly averted a strike of 660 armored car drivers, messengers,

and vault guards in Chicago. The Teamsters Union wanted a raise of 12 cents an hour for the first year, 8 cents for the second year, and 10 cents for the third year in its three-year contract, but the companies would not agree to that. The dispute went into mediation, and a compromise was reached at the 11th hour, thanks in part to the looming threat of hundreds of banks and currency exchanges in the city going without armored-car transport the following day.[46]

Tensions ran higher 11 years later, when 700 Brink's and Purolator guards went on strike for three days after contract negotiations failed. During the strike, businesses, banks, and government offices were forced to move securities and cash without armored car protection.[47] Chicago police and the Cook County sheriff guarded city and county funds being taken to banks, but police refused private requests to move money, and banks were forced to set up alternate arrangements.[48]

The 1977 Teamsters strike in New York, which lasted nine weeks, affected all three major

Brink's smallest truck, shown here in a 1970 photo, was designed especially for Chicago parking garages with low ceilings. *(Photo courtesy of Wisconsin Historical Society #WHi-28405.)*

THE STATE OF CASH

FOR YEARS WE'VE BEEN HEARING ABOUT THE "cashless" society, one in which we'll pay for all our goods with plastic, over the Internet, or perhaps with our cell phones or a microchip implanted in our necks.

Although there is little doubt that electronic payments have enjoyed explosive growth, the idea of a cashless society, at least for the foreseeable future, is about as likely as the paperless office.

According to the Federal Reserve Bank of San Francisco, the value of U.S. currency in circulation has been climbing steadily from $93.4 billion in 1977 to $783.2 billion in 2006 and cash accounts for two-thirds of personal payments in the United States—of course, that's just what we know about. Cash is not trackable, so this number could be even higher.

The reason cash maintains its place in our selection of payment options is simple. There is no single payment device that can mimic the convenience, anonymity, flexibility, and ubiquity of cash.

---

armored car operators—Brink's, Wells Fargo, and Purolator. The union demanded a 26 percent pay raise as well as increased benefits. In the end, the companies agreed to most of the union's demands.[49]

Moving Beyond Cash

In 1970, to finance further expansion, Pittston publicly offered 500,000 shares of Brink's common stock—the first such offering since Pittston had gained full control over Brink's. In May 1972, Pittston offered a 2-for-1 stock split. Brink's shares then totaled 10 million.[50]

The company also had plans to expand the air courier service and planned to enter into the security patrol business, hiring out armored cars and crews to look after branch banks and other financial establishments during non-business hours.

In addition, CEO Edgar Jones told the *Chicago Tribune* that Brink's was also considering "the manufacture and possibly the marketing of a specific burglar alarm system" in response to an industry in transition due to the decline in cash payrolls and check-cashing services. "Handling of currency,

as far as counting and packing goes, is a dying business," he added.[51]

Despite its far-flung business ventures, Brink's had not forgotten its roots. "It doesn't matter where you came from, what college degree you had—you started on the trucks as a guard, and then you got to drive and [be a] messenger," said Ron Muir, a 41-year Brink's employee.[52]

Frank Lennon, Brink's vice president and chief administrative officer, came to Pittston in 1977. He added, "I would say that Brink's had its own separate and distinct and readily identifiable culture that was very different from the Pittston culture. The Brink's culture was really nourished as a separate and distinct culture and eventually that culture became the prevailing culture [at Pittston]."[53]

With the expanded company showing gains in 1973, Pittston started buying up common shares again. In 1978, it bought 1.2 million more publicly traded shares at $9.63 per share. It then owned 99 percent of Brink's.[54]

In June 1979, the Interstate Commerce Commission approved Brink's merger with Pittston, and Pittston purchased the remaining 1 percent of shares.[55]

Brink's returned to Australia in 1987 under its own name after an unsuccessful venture with local company Brambles Industries Limited. *(Photo courtesy of Brink's Museum.)*

CHAPTER EIGHT

A SUCCESSFUL TURNAROUND

1980–1989

All of a sudden, the U.S. operation went from losing money, to making money.

—Brink's President and CEO Michael Dan[1]

BRINK'S FACED MULTIPLE CHALLENGES in the 1980s. Its parent company, Pittston, had overextended itself during the 1970s in response to the rising price of coal. "We were getting, at times, 100 bucks a ton or more for our product, and we were one of the largest natural resources companies in the country," said Jim Spurlock, a vice president at The Pittston Coal Company beginning in 1977. "I think we were maybe, at one point in time, fifth or sixth. We had about 20,000 rank-and-file organized coal miners working for us. So it was a pretty exciting place."[2]

However, by the early 1980s, coal prices dropped dramatically as export volumes plummeted and the demand for metallurgical coal, Pittston's specialty, fell especially low when steel plants across the world began to operate below capacity. "Coal is a horror story in terms of demand," analyst Joel Price told the *New York Times* in 1983.[3]

"As the largest exporter of domestic coal ... Pittston has suffered," stated another *New York Times* article in 1984. "The company showed a deficit in 1982, and its directors recently eliminated the common-stock dividend."[4]

According to Brink's future U.S. Chief Financial Officer John Hague, who worked in Pittston's accounting department at the time, eventually

Pittston was selling coal for around "what it was costing them to pull it out of the ground."[5]

From 1982 to 1987, Pittston posted four annual net losses, including a $17.3 million loss in 1982. Brink's President and CEO Michael Dan, who started working at Brink's in 1982, recalled:

They had the best coal in the world, and they were shipping it all to Japan. The price of coal goes up; the price of coal comes down. They'd come through the 1970s, [which were] boom times, and they made so much money. You can look at this in the annual reports. ...

They took all the money and bought several other coal companies, thinking coal prices were always going to stay that high. Well, of course, they collapsed and stayed down for 20 years. So they had over-expanded. They bought a bunch of properties at a high price. When the coal price fell, it fell from $100 a ton in 1982. By 1983 to 1984, it was probably $30.

We went from 22,000 employees to 2,000 employees in four years.[6]

Michael T. Dan joined Brink's in 1982, and in 1991, became its president. *(Photo courtesy of Brink's Museum.)*

At the same time, the petroleum distribution side of the company's holdings, based in Canada and the United States, was performing poorly, with a world oil glut driving down prices. Pittston sold off Pittston Petroleum in 1982 and used the revenue to purchase Burlington Northern Air Freight from Burlington Northern Railroad for $177 million. After the sale, the company was renamed Burlington Air Express (BAX), and later, BAX Global, Inc. Unlike Air Courier, which specialized in transporting money and valuables, BAX served as a general heavy freight express carrier.[7]

Because of those differences, little overlap existed between Brink's Air Courier and Burlington Air Express—and because Pittston regarded Brink's mainly as a moneymaking side interest, executives decided that the companies would share few resources. "We were never really able to utilize their network to work our services," explained John Hague, retired Brink's U.S. chief financial officer.[8]

Unfortunately, the BAX acquisition also suffered from bad timing. New changes in federal air pollution rules forced passenger airlines to retire older aircraft. Prior to the changes, BAX mainly relied on rented spaces in such aircraft during overnight flights, and the company found itself with few alternative transportation options.

The situation forced BAX to buy its own aircraft, a major unforeseen expense that required a much greater capital investment than Pittston executives could have anticipated.

"Before that, you were using American Airlines' assets or Eastern's assets," Dan said. "You were just paying so much to put your freight on board. It destroyed the company."[9]

Some of those losses were offset by Brink's success in expanding into new markets. In 1983, Brink's branched out into the consumer market with Brink's Home Security (BHS), a burglar and fire alarm company launched in Portland, Oregon.

1981

Members of the Weather Underground terrorist group kill a Brink's guard and two policemen during a robbery.

1983

Brink's Home Security is founded in Portland, Oregon.

BRINK'S MUSEUM

BAX GLOBAL

1982

Brink's buys Burlington Northern Air Freight express mail service from Burlington Northern Railroad.

In 1983, Brink's Home Security was founded in Portland, Oregon. By 1985, it had expanded to several other cities. *(Photo courtesy of Brink's Museum.)*

By 1986, the subsidiary had 17 branches around the United States, served approximately 25,000 homes, and planned to expand to 56 U.S. cities. It proved successful enough to require the subsidiary to relocate to a new 56,000-square-foot facility in Carrollton, Texas, to house the BHS National Support and Monitoring Center.[10]

Brazen Robberies

In July 1980, Brink's suffered a record-shattering incident of employee theft. Brink's employee Rick Douglas Cunningham failed to show up for work in the "gold room" at the Los Angeles branch, where he worked as one of five guards. An audit four days later revealed that 2,250 South African gold coins—$1.5 million in Krugerrands—were missing.

The Los Angeles Police Department determined that Cunningham likely stole the coins in small amounts over a period of three months.

1985
The company's new official magazine *Brink's Link* debuts.

BRINK'S MUSEUM

BRINK'S MUSEUM

1984
Future CEO Michael Dan, then vice president of operations, begins decertifying the Teamsters Union in Brink's branches throughout the country.

1989
Despite several years of declining revenues throughout the decade, Brink's ends the decade with a return to profitability.

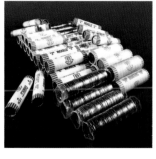

BRINK'S MUSEUM

THE WEATHER UNDERGROUND ROBBERY

AT APPROXIMATELY 4 P.M. ON OCTOBER 20, 1981, three gunmen jumped from a red van and opened fire on three Brink's guards making a pickup at the Nanuet National Bank in Rockland County, New York. Peter Paige, a 49-year-old guard, was killed instantly by a shot to the throat. His partner, 48-year-old Francis Joseph Trombino, suffered critical injuries from a bullet that severed an artery in his arm.

The gunmen fled in a U-Haul with $1.6 million. "They didn't even ask [the guards] to hand over the money," recalled a stunned witness to the robbery. "They just blasted away."[1]

After traveling approximately three miles, the U-Haul hit a police roadblock at an entrance to the New York State Thruway. The police stopped the truck, guns drawn. A woman jumped out of the cab, arms raised, and begged police to drop their guns. Reluctantly, they did, just as six men with submachine guns "burst out of the truck and opened fire," according to the *New York Times*.[2] Sgt. Edward O'Grady and Waverly Brown, both police officers, died in the shooting.[3]

Four robbers were arrested on the scene; others fled in a second getaway car, but were later arrested. The story took a dramatic turn after the

---

They were unable to solve the crime, however. Cunningham—and the Krugerrands—have never been found.[11]

Shortly after the Krugerrand theft, part-time Brink's guard George Bosque disappeared with $1.85 million and a Brink's van after a pickup of bank money at San Francisco International Airport. He then abandoned the van and skipped town in a car belonging to a maid at a nearby hotel.[12]

When the van did not show up for its next appointment at the Federal Reserve Bank of San Francisco, the authorities began searching for Bosque. A former neighbor mentioned that Bosque

Brink's "gold room" employee Rick Douglas Cunningham (left) likely made off with $1.5 million in Krugerrands, while guard George M. Bosque (right) stole a Brink's truck containing $1.85 million. *(Photo courtesy of Brink's Museum.)*

REWARD

$50,000.⁰⁰

for information leading to the arrest of RICK D. CUNNINGHAM, Brea, California, based on a felony arrest warrant issued by the Los Angeles Police Department which relates to the theft of gold Krugerrands from Brink's, Incorporated, Los Angeles, California on or about June 25, 1980.

Any persons having any such information should contact the Los Angeles Police Department, Lt. Armas, telephone number (213) 485-4073 or the Federal Bureau of Investigation, telephone number (213) 272-6161, or Brink's, Incorporated, Mr. Curnutt, telephone number (213) 749-1757.

$50,000.⁰⁰

for information leading to the arrest of GEORGE M. BOSQUE, San Francisco, California, based on a felony arrest warrant which relates to a theft of currency from a Brink's armored truck on August 15, 1980.

Any persons having any such information should contact the Federal Bureau of Investigation, telephone number (415) 552-2155 or Brink's, Incorporated, Mr. Curnutt, telephone number (213) 749-1757.

$150,000.⁰⁰

A separate reward of $150,000 will be paid for information which leads to the recovery of the 2,250 Krugerrands or the $1,850,000. A partial recovery of either the gold coins or $1,850,000 will be paid on a pro rata basis.

All information will be treated confidentially. In case of a duplication of information or dispute, the Board of Directors of Brink's, Incorporated shall be the sole judge as to whom the reward shall be paid or as to the manner in which the reward may be divided. These rewards shall supercede and cancel any previously issued rewards relating to the above thefts and shall be cancelled on and after December 31, 1980.

Brink's, Incorporated Darien, Connecticut 06820

four robbers were fingerprinted. The woman who pleaded with police to put down their guns was 38-year-old Kathy Boudin, a member of the Weather Underground, originally known as the Weathermen. The group had claimed responsibility for bombing the Pentagon and the U.S. Capitol, as well as courthouses and banks, in protest of U.S. involvement in the Vietnam War.

Boudin first made news in 1961 after she survived an explosion in a townhouse in New York's Greenwich Village. Three members of the Weather Underground had been downstairs making a bomb, which exploded for unknown reasons. All three died. Fellow Weatherman Cathlyn Wilkerson escaped with Boudin after being rescued by policemen who entered the burning structure in search of survivors.[4]

Boudin made the FBI's Most Wanted List for her participation in the 1969 Chicago "Days of Rage"—a Vietnam War protest marked by extreme vandalism, bombings, and violence.

By the time of the 1981 robbery, Boudin no longer faced federal charges, but was still wanted in Illinois for jumping bail.[5] She had been living in New York with her 1-year-old son, Chesa, collecting welfare benefits under the alias Lynn Adams.[6] Chesa's father was David Gilbert, a member of the Black Liberation Army—a 1960s radical group and offshoot of the Black Panthers.

Six members of the Black Liberation Army, including Gilbert, were involved in the Brink's robbery. "Except for the murderous fusillades, the botched Brink's job seemed a routine case," observed *Time* magazine. "But as police and federal agents began to examine it closely, they found themselves back in the 1960s rummaging through the ... catacombs of Vietnam-era radicals."[7]

Gilbert and two other men received three consecutive 25-years-to-life sentences for killing a police officer. Three others received sentences ranging from 50 to 75 years.

Boudin plead guilty to first-degree robbery and second-degree murder and was sentenced to 25 years to life. When she was up for parole in 2001, Paige's son told the parole board, "No matter what her role was, she was part of a planned terrorist attack. My family and other families suffer every day for this."[8] Her parole was denied.

had recently suffered two epileptic seizures and was worried that if Brink's found out, he would lose his job because he would no longer be able to carry a gun.[13]

Bosque remained at large for 18 months, racing to spend the money as fast as possible.[14] He dropped $100,000 to produce a pornographic film called *Centurions of Rome* while living in penthouse suites and traveling in rented limousines, helicopters, and cabin cruisers.[15] He spent $60,000 "to furnish and decorate a $1,160-a-month apartment in Greenwich Village in 'opulent Art Deco style,'" according to the *New York Times*, sent large sums to friends, and even donated $10,000 to the San Francisco Society for the Prevention of Cruelty to Animals.[16]

Bosque was finally captured after a friend seeking the $500,000 reward called police.[17] He had just $100 in his pocket when he was arrested as he stepped out of a phone booth at a San Francisco supermarket parking lot.[18]

Bosque plead guilty to the crime and was sentenced to 15 years in prison. In 1986, he was released on parole. Five years after his release, he was found dead in his apartment, possibly of a drug overdose. Cocaine and narcotics paraphernalia were found at the scene.[19]

Although no customers lost a penny due to these criminal activities, Brink's was quick to react, tightening internal controls and security processes. "We simply cannot tolerate criminal behavior from our employees," says Bruce Woerner, security directory for Brink's operations in the United States. "We continue to be on the forefront of pre-employment screening and employee criminal background check technology. We also review and update internal processes on an ongoing basis, always mindful of our obligation to protect our customers' cash and valuables, and to bring our people home safely each and every night."

Above: Gary K. Garton joined Brink's as president in 1985.

Below right: Hobart K. Robinson became Brink's president in 1980, after spending seven years at the McKinsey & Co. professional services firm. *(Photos courtesy of Brink's Museum.)*

Pittston's Cash Cow

Most Pittston executives felt little emotional attachment to the armored-car industry, according to Jim Spurlock, regarding Brink's mostly as a ready source of liquidity. "Brink's performed well for Pittston," Spurlock admitted. "Even in the heyday when coal was a hundred bucks a ton, Brink's was still supplying cash for [Pittston's] operations and expansion."[20]

According to John Hague, "Brink's has always been a strong company. It's a service business, and I think [Pittston] used it to expand and grow the coal business."[21]

During the coal slump, Pittston's board of directors made plans to sell off Brink's in an effort to raise cash. Pittston considered Brambles Industries Limited, Australia's largest armored car company and a partner of Brink's for a short time in the 1970s, a top contender for the sale. Brambles had

even started making plans to send top executive Gary Garton to the United States to run Brink's.[22]

However, Brambles faced its own problems at the time. Media mogul Rupert Murdoch announced his intentions to buy out its biggest shareholder and take over the company. "They had to borrow a bunch of money to get rid of him, and they pulled out of the acquisition," Dan explained.[23]

According to Dan, Pittston made the decision to sell without consulting Brink's President Hobart K. Robinson. When Robinson found out "they weren't being honest with him, he quit and walked out at the end of 1984," Dan recalled.

Six months later, Gary Garton stepped in to serve as Brink's new president.

A Global Reach

Brink's expanded its international operations to India in 1981, forming a startup security company in partnership with a transportation and logistics company based in India.

According to Krishna Kotak, managing director of Brink's India:

India was just getting into the global diamond cutting and polishing field. Up to then,

Belgium and Israel were really the countries which were substantial in doing that business. India was making rapid strides, and I think a lot of Brink's customers, especially in the United States, said it would be good if you had a footprint in India.[24]

Above: Brink's Arya is the company's affiliate in India.

Below: Brink's established an affiliate in Thailand in 1986. *(Photos courtesy of Brink's Museum.)*

Under Garton's leadership, Brink's branched out even further across the globe to Bangkok, Thailand, and Seoul, South Korea.

The company selected Bangkok because of its prominence as a cutting and processing center for rubies and sapphires mined in nearby provinces. The small venture involved just two armored trucks operating out of a facility in the heart of the gem district.[25]

South Korea proved attractive because of its growing economy and its capital's burgeoning reputation as an international city. Brink's wanted to establish a presence in Southeast Asia, and Seoul, South Korea, scheduled to host the 1988 Olympics, seemed the ideal place to start.[26]

Brink's also became interested in expanding into the Japanese market. In 1986, Brink's Air Courier moved $6 billion in gold bullion from New York to the Japanese mint in Osaka, where it was used to mint coins honoring the 60th anniversary of the reign of Japanese Emperor Hirohito.

The shipment was one of the most valuable in Brink's history, "of such a magnitude that it required mentioning by the U.S. government in the balance of trade statistics for June to make the statistics meaningful for the month," as noted in *Brink's Link*.[27]

Japan's jewelry market was large and growing, second in size only to that of the United States, making it an ideal addition to the Brink's Diamond & Jewelry Network. At the time, Brink's was using Nippon Express for shipments throughout Japan. Although it was the largest express company in the nation, Nippon Express had met its match in rival company Jewelry Trade Center (JTC). Run by a former customs officer, JTC held a special advantage over other diamond and jewelry couriers in Japan. Only JTC had a permit to take diamonds from the terminal to a bonded warehouse where customers could view the shipments before accepting them, thus bypassing the sale—and the taxes—in the event the diamonds did not meet their needs.

Joseph Eyal, a tenacious Israeli who spent 26 years in his country's military before joining Brink's, was developing the burgeoning Brink's Diamond & Jewelry Network and was not to be deterred by JTC. When JTC refused to deal with him, Eyal looked to his own global network of business contacts to arrange introductions to Japanese companies. Within a short time, Brink's entered into a joint venture, obtained the proper licenses, and began offering the same bonded warehouse privileges to Brink's customers.

Brink's had tried and failed in the past to get the same privileges. "They were told, 'That's impossible,'" said Eyal. "But everything is possible to an Israeli military man. We fixed it."[28]

An International Incident

In 1985, $8 million worth of $100 bills was discovered missing at the Buenos Aires Airport in Argentina. The bills were part of a $50 million Air Courier shipment from the Federal Reserve Bank of New York to the Central Bank of Argentina. The shipment consisted of 11 bags of $4 million each and two bags of $3 million each. Robert DeNisco, the air courier who in 1977 had single-handedly thwarted a hijacking, checked in the bags as his personal luggage.

When members of the Argentine military picked up the shipment, they found two bags missing.[29]

Above left: Air courier service was an important component of Brink's Israel.

Below: Joseph Eyal, founder and current chairman of Brink's Global Services, is shown here in 2000 with his wife, Batia Eyal. *(Photos courtesy of Brink's Museum.)*

In 1986, Air Courier transported $6 billion in gold bullion from New York to Japan. *(Photo courtesy of Brink's Museum.)*

For six weeks, the circumstances surrounding the missing bags remained a mystery. The incident was still being called a "loss" of baggage, but "fears are growing that they were stolen from Rio de Janeiro National Airport," where the plane had a two-hour layover, reported the *New York Times*.

Brazilian drug enforcement authorities finally found the money after tracing the serial numbers to one of the thieves, who had used some of the bills to purchase drugs. Upon questioning, they learned that the thieves had been temporary workers at the Rio de Janeiro airport and initially thought they were stealing suitcases full of music cassettes.[30]

An Independent Streak

From 1940 to 1980, competition in the U.S. trucking industry remained limited by the Interstate Commerce Committee's (ICC) reluctance to grant licenses to new trucking companies. If a new carrier proposed a service that existing carriers were not offering, the ICC preferred to give existing firms the first crack at providing that service, rather than licensing a new company. As a result, typically, the only way for a new carrier to enter the market was by purchasing the rights of an established carrier.[31]

However, the transportation marketplace changed after President Jimmy Carter signed the Motor Carrier Act of 1980 into law. The new law, according to economist Thomas Gale Moore, made the certification process "significantly easier" for new trucking companies. It eliminated most restrictions on goods, routes, and geographic regions of the country and gave carriers more freedom in pricing.[32]

Between 1980 and 1990, the number of trucking firms in the United States more than doubled, to more than 40,000 by 1990.[33] This new openness also brought about the proliferation of nonunion shops. "Deregulation has made it easier for nonunion

MICHAEL T. DAN

MICHAEL T. DAN, A CHICAGO BOY WHO FIXED up and raced dragsters in his spare time, went to community college for automotive design, and by age 29 had become the head of Armored Vehicle Builders in Pittsfield, Massachusetts.[1]

Like fellow South Side Chicagoan J. D. Allen two generations before, Dan was a bright, enterprising young man who made up in vision what he lacked in formal education."[2] In 1980, Brink's President Bart Robinson met Dan at the National Armored Car Association's annual convention and offered him a position at Brink's. Robinson had been seeking someone with truck expertise to help standardize operations internationally and reduce costs. "The company was in serious trouble financially," Dan recalled. "Trucks were our biggest capital expenditure at that time."[3]

Two years later, in 1982, Dan agreed to work for Brink's as the director of automotive design. It was not a smooth transition. "I hated my job," Dan admitted. "I'd always been run-ning the business before, and I hated being the staff guy."

However, Robinson had a reason for placing Dan in the position—he wanted Dan to learn about operations before moving up the ranks.[4] By February 1984, Dan was promoted to vice president of operations for the western region of the United States. His first task was to decertify the Teamsters, which under the Taft-Hartley Act of 1947 technically served at the pleasure of Brink's. Pressure to disengage from the union had mounted in the 1970s and early 1980s as industry deregulation allowed small start-up armored car companies to hire non-union workers for low wages. Brink's wage costs, and thus its rates, rose so high in comparison that it lost clients and became unable to compete with the smaller companies.[5] "I was sent out there for a three-year assignment to fix the West Coast," Dan explained. Worker affinity for the Teamsters was at a low point, so Dan was able to decertify six branches—Seattle, Oakland, San Francisco, Sacramento, Los

workers to get jobs in the trucking industry," Moore explained. "This new competition has sharply eroded the strength of the Teamsters."

In a stark example of that evolution, during the late 1970s, 60 percent of all jobs in the trucking industry were union—by 1985, only 28 percent were union.[34] The International Brotherhood of Teamsters continued to represent Brink's drivers. This situation left Brink's at a significant disadvantage. Dan served as the head of Brink's West Coast operations in 1984. He explained:

> We had competitors literally having two guys on a truck, paying them $5 an hour between both of them. And we had Teamsters we were paying $13 an hour, $12 an hour, and Teamster benefit plans. ... Our hourly cost per truck was a significant multiple.

> To give you a flavor of what happened, there was a company called Purolator Courier ... and they started an armored car company. They'd build a branch in town. Not even call on a customer—they'd send a letter: "We're new in town. We're Purolator Company, and we will do your Brink's work." Attach a copy of the Brink's contract. Take off 50 percent. "That's our price."[35]

Added Jeff Pagano, Brink's counsel in union matters in 1984:

> Brink's marketed itself to its customers, [convincing] the customers that they ought to use Brink's service because 77 cents of every dollar of revenue generated went to employees. So if you know anything about anything in terms of

Angeles, and San Diego—in 30 days. Within a year, he completed decertification of the West Coast and was promoted to director of North American operations.[6]

In 1991, Dan was chosen to head Brink's Worldwide and placed in charge of improving the lackluster performance of Brink's international affiliates. Brink's typically had part ownership in these affiliates, partnering with security or transport companies that were already established in each country. "We owned shares in all these companies, and they wouldn't pay any attention to us," Dan recalled. "So I started getting on an airplane and flying around and trying to figure out what to do with the rest of the Brink's world. It was not doing well, and I made a decision."[7]

He gave the affiliates an ultimatum—either sell 100 percent to Brink's, or Brink's would exit the partnership entirely. "'You buy me, or I am buying you,'" he said. "The reality is they couldn't believe that I would leave because their whole franchise was built up around the brand name."[8]

Most opted to sell to Brink's. A few, including Italian affiliate Brink's SecureMark, chose instead to surrender the widely recognized Brink's name and strike out on their own. Most eventually failed.[9]

Dan rose to chairman and CEO of Pittston in 1998, leading the effort to sell off the company's unprofitable natural resources holdings. In 2003, a much more streamlined version of Pittston officially became The Brink's Company. Under his leadership, the transition brought Brink's back to its roots and left the company in a position to increase its profits in the long term.

labor, you realize that there's no company that succeeds if 77 percent of revenue is going to labor. While it's a nice thing in a very charitable way, it means there's not enough money to pay for refurbishing trucks, facilities, management, etc. So that was a message to the world that they had a problem.[36]

Pittston had already taken steps to decertify the union in two cities. However, when workers in New York went on strike in the early 1980s, Pittston stopped the decertification process. With coal prices down, Pittston did not want to add strike expenses and liabilities for unfunded pensions to its financial burden.

"If you throw the Teamsters out, you've got to pay your share of that," said Dan. "That was a big tab. But I was convinced that we had no way to survive if we didn't continue decertification of the Teamsters."[37]

He started with the West Coast. The union was particularly strong there, and Pittston worried about a strike, but the decertification went through without any work stoppage. Brink's had the Taft-Hartley Act of 1947 on its side. The law outlawed armed security guards from joining a union that represented other types of employees, such as the Teamsters, allowing Brink's to decertify the union at its discretion.[38]

In a month's time, Dan and his crew were able to decertify the Teamsters in Seattle, Oakland, San Francisco, Sacramento, Los Angeles, and San Diego. "We had one little labor disruption a year later, at one branch," Dan recalled. "That's it."

According to Gary Taylor, Brink's vice president of international operations and a 30-year employee,

Above: Brink's Singapore was launched in 1989.

Below left and right: Brink's Coin Processing Network was equipped to wrap more than 30 million coin rolls a month. *(Photos courtesy of Brink's Museum.)*

"I think that process was without question a huge turning point in the company. It was an unbelievable strategic move."

Impressed by the swiftness of the process, Pittston then gave Dan the go-ahead to decertify the rest of the U.S. branches, putting forth $18 million to finance the unfunded union pension funds. With the Teamsters out, "all of a sudden, the U.S. operation went from losing money to making money," said Dan.[39]

Along with the decertification, Brink's also made several changes designed to benefit the company overall, including the divestment of the small truck leasing side of the business for $14.8 million, and efforts to computerize the branches.

At the same time, Brink's newly implemented Speak Out Sessions encouraged employees to suggest changes in operations and alerted Brink's management to problems at the branches that might have otherwise gone overlooked. In Detroit, Michigan; Kansas City, Missouri; and Chicago, Illinois, the lack of training for new employees proved a major concern among the staff. Management

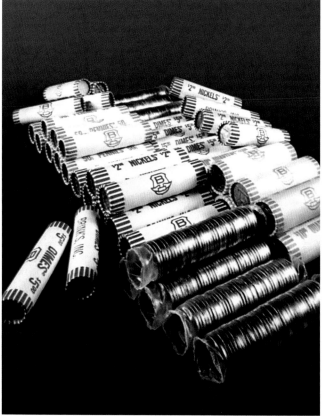

This 1981 Brink's truck hailed from France. *(Photo courtesy of Brink's Museum.)*

responded by partnering up new and longtime employees on crews and introducing training videos to the company orientation program.[40]

"For the first time, we have reversed the revenue decline which began approximately five years ago," Dan wrote in the Winter 1987 issue of *Brink's Link*. He spoke optimistically of a profit-sharing plan that rewarded success within individual branches and told employees to look sharp. "It's time to clean up our branches, repaint our trucks, and improve our appearance," he added.[41]

Brink's invested in new operating facilities for St. Louis, Missouri, and Fort Lauderdale, Florida, as well as its Washington, D.C., coinsorting operation, and expanded its armored-truck facilities in Los Angeles. It also opened a new training center in Richmond, Virginia.[42] Overseas, Brink's bought out VGL Security in France, an armored-car firm with 500 workers and 160 vehicles.[43]

It also made overtures to acquire competitor Loomis Corp. The stalwart of the armored-car business in the South and parts of the Pacific Northwest, it had a history almost as long as Brink's.[44]

The impending merger of two big names in the armored car industry caught the attention of the U.S. Justice Department, however. James F. Rill, the new head of the U.S. Antitrust Division, filed a lawsuit against the proposed merger, prompting the two companies to call off the deal.[45]

Although Brink's faced major challenges in the 1980s, the company ended the decade profitably. More important, it had strong leadership in place to lead the company to success in an increasingly global society.

This photo from the 1990s shows a truck from Brink's Italy. Brink's ultimately divested itself of its Italian affiliate and formed a new venture in Arezzo, Italy. *(Photo courtesy of REPETTI S.r.l.)*

CHAPTER NINE

INTERNATIONAL GROWTH

1990–2000

I remember [future CEO Michael] Dan saying 10 years ago in a meeting that our intention is to change the company from an international company into a global company. I am a very strong believer in that.

—Haim Zanzer,
Brink's vice president
of information systems[1]

WITH NORTH AMERICAN OPERA-tions successfully stream-lined, Brink's executives turned their attention to the company's international interests—a patchwork of partial and minority ownership ventures. "Growth had been inconsistent from country to country, since local partners handled operations with little corporate oversight. The operators of the business … were basically serving themselves and not running the business," said future CEO Michael Dan, who served as head of Brink's Worldwide during the 1990s.[2]

By now, Brink's had a vision—and a plan—to transform the company from a U.S. organization with international operations to a truly global entity. "Our customers were increasingly global, and we intended to serve their needs wherever they did business, and with the same level of security, service, and trust they expected from Brink's," explained Dan.

To put the plan in motion, Dan instituted a policy of purchasing controlling interests in international affiliates whenever possible and dissolving or selling any joint venture that refused to cooperate. "I would show up [and say,] 'Hello, I'm Michael Dan. … Here's how I want to run the company,'" he recalled.[3] "This policy gave the company the control it needed to ensure consistency of service and to begin the process of building a cohesive global entity

with which to serve its customers worldwide.

In Europe, consistency proved especially crucial. At the time, the region had started the shift to a common currency, the euro, and Brink's wanted to be ready to serve those companies that would soon be expanding in response to new financial and competitive opportunities across and beyond the Eurozone. In 1990, Brink's bought the remaining 65 percent of shares of Brink's-MAT armored car and air courier operations in the United Kingdom, which totaled $65 million in combined annual revenues. As part of the agreement, Brink's gained at least 50 percent ownership interests in Brink's affiliates in Belgium, Germany, Holland, Ireland, Bahrain, and Hong Kong, with 100 percent ownership in Switzerland.[4] The company's international growth plan was officially in motion.

The Birth of Brink's Global Services

In Italy, Brink's encountered an even greater opportunity—one that had been simmering for

---

Brink's established operations in Greece in 1995. *(Photo courtesy of Brink's Museum.)*

many months. Already a 24.5 percent owner in the Brink's SecureMark partnership, the company offered its signature cash-in-transit service throughout the country. Brink's executives, however, had other ideas. According to Joseph Eyal, founder and chairman of Brink's Global Services, "Italy was a main producer of jewelry at that time, with huge volumes coming into the country and going out to the U.S. and other places. Small secure transportation companies could handle pieces of the business, but there was no international company to fill the logistics void."

In 1992, Brink's formed a diamond and jewelry company, subcontracting all but the administrative work. While the new company brought cohesion and a single point of contact to customers that otherwise would have had to deal with multiple companies for each shipment, the venture was not meeting Brink's service standards. Due to operational limitations, these smaller companies could move the jewelry only part of the way.

Trucks would pick up from Arezzo, near Florence, or from Vicenza, near Venice, and cross the border into Switzerland, where the jewelry would be loaded onto different trucks and taken to the airport, then loaded on a plane bound for the United States or other parts of the world. "The process was inefficient. Trucks would be delayed in traffic or bad weather, and the various transitions increased risk. We needed a way to move jewelry securely, without interruption," said Eyal.

From this need, the next generation of global secure logistics was born. Working with the strongest of the small transportation companies in Italy, Brink's created a new company, based in Arezzo, to transport shipments directly from the pickup location to the airport. Brink's then struck a deal with Lufthansa Airlines to ship jewelry directly from Italy. The organization grew quickly, capturing the lion's share of Italy's diamond and jewelry transportation business within a few short years. Explained Eyal, "When we first approached

1990
Future CEO Michael Dan leads Brink's in instituting a policy of obtaining controlling interests in its international affiliates.

BRINK'S MUSEUM

1993
Brink's launches joint ventures in El Salvador, Luxembourg, and Taiwan.

BRINK'S MUSEUM

BRINK'S MUSEUM

1990
Brink's acquires all outstanding shares of its Brink's-MAT affiliate in the United Kingdom, a major step toward strengthening the company's European operations.

1993
Wynne Berry, director of operations and security for Brink's Global Services, begins to lay the groundwork for Brink's expansion into Eastern Europe.

BRINK'S MUSEUM

Lufthansa, we estimated our shipping volume would be 80 kilos to 200 kilos, maybe 400. Within a few months, we were shipping 10 tons a week."

In Belgium, Brink's had a 50 percent interest in Brink's Ziegler, the biggest freight company in the country. While this gave the company a strong presence in the market, Brink's executives sensed an even bigger opportunity—an office in Antwerp, the diamond center of the world, where billions of dollars worth of the jewels shipped in and out on a routine basis. Unconvinced that the company could successfully break into the tightly established network in Antwerp, executives at Ziegler refused to participate and eventually sold their interest in the diamond transportation activities to Brink's. In 1991, Brink's opened its Antwerp office under the name Brink's Diamond Jewelry Service.

At that time, diamond dealers were struggling with the high cost of borrowing money to fund their exports. Brink's contracted with a small company in Antwerp, named EDS, that was handling the

Guard dogs occasionally accompany Brink's crews in Belgium. *(Photo courtesy of Brink's Museum.)*

documentation on behalf of the diamond dealers, thus lowering their cost. The company convinced the Bank of India to let them manage their documentation activities. As a result of the joint effort between

1995
Brink's opens its first branch in Eastern Europe with the launching of its operations in Russia.

BRINK'S MUSEUM

1997
Brink's launches its largest start-up yet, in Argentina.

BRINK'S MUSEUM

BRINK'S MUSEUM

1995
Brink's CompuSafe® is introduced.

1999
In an effort to streamline its operations, Brink's consolidates its management structure.

Brink's and EDS, Brink's annual revenues from its Antwerp business quintupled.[5]

"[Antwerp] has turned out to a very, very successful operation that generates a lot of revenue and also helps extend the footprint that we have around the globe," said Gabi Ben-Harosh, vice president of finance for Brink's Global Services.

Full ownership in Switzerland gave Brink's a foothold with important banking and precious metals clients. "For centuries, many of the important refineries of precious metals in the world have been Swiss refineries," said Gilad Glaser, general manager of Brink's Switzerland. "The Swiss banks on the banknote side are still players as well, just by the virtue of being Swiss banks."

In Hong Kong, Brink's controlling interests gave the company more strength in decision-making. "For too many years, there was not really the proper kind of attention that really worked as a group for the benefit of Brink's," said Erez Weiss, operations head of Brink's Hong Kong since 1993. "I went to Hong Kong, and Brink's Global Services' Joseph Eyal actually brought some of his 'soldiers,'

Above right: Brink's established its affiliate in Taiwan in 1993.

Above left: Brink's established operations in Luxembourg in 1993; the Luxembourg headquarters is shown here.

Below left: Kristina Chen (right), the general manager of Brink's Taiwan, is shown here in 2000 with Rainbow Wang of Brink's Hong Kong. *(Photos courtesy of Brink's Museum.)*

as we call them. They grouped together and gave orders and provided all the facility and support for building a true global business for diamonds and jewelry first, and then a few years later, we did the commodities."[6]

Since that time, "from a commercial and business standpoint, there have not been any real major changes in Hong Kong at all," said Guy Bullen, who joined Brink's Asia in 1994. "During the British handover to China during 1996 and 1997, the commercial activity in Hong Kong and the tourist activity and the amount of buzz in the air was quite electric. There was certainly a feeling among the people living here, locals and expatriates and also people that were traveling here, that history was in the making and that it was a very special time. From a business standpoint, there was a lot going on. Economically, there was a lot of money moving around, and from a personal standpoint, it certainly was a very, very interesting time to be here, to be present for that."[7]

In a few countries, Brink's decided to keep things as they were. "We're still minority in Peru, India, and Thailand," said Dan. "If we have good partners, I don't have a problem with that."[8]

Across the Globe and Back Again

As Brink's reorganized its existing international affiliates, it also extended its reach to more countries. In 1993, the company launched ventures in El Salvador, Luxembourg, and Taiwan. "I remember Mr. Dan saying 10 years ago in a meeting that our intention is to change the company from an international company into a global company, and I am a very strong believer in that," said Haim Zanzer, Brink's vice president of information systems.[9]

According to Kristina Chen, general manager of Brink's Taiwan, the Taiwan branch was created at the request of Bank of America, a global customer with operations in the country. At first, Brink's partnered with a local security company, which hired the crews and owned the trucks. However, the partner soon faced financial problems. According to Chen:

> They basically focused on local guarding services, while Brink's focused on global services. They just had a different approach on how to develop security servicing in this market. They thought they could get their return from the investment quickly, within a year or two.[10]

As a result, the relationship soon ended, and Brink's acquired its own crews and trucks.

Brink's gained new footholds in 1993. Wynne Berry, director of operations and security for Brink's Global Services, laid the groundwork for the com-

Above: Wynne Berry (left), Brink's director of operations and security for Brink's Global Services, helped establish Brink's in Eastern Europe. He stands with Guy Bullen of Brink's Asia Pacific operations.

Below left: Brink's established operations in Russia in 1995. *(Photos courtesy of Brink's Museum.)*

pany's business ventures in Russia and other former Soviet states. He met with Russian officials in Georgia who oversaw the region's security and communications systems. At the time, Georgia was in the midst of a civil war. The first democratically elected president of Georgia had been overthrown in a military coup in 1992—an attempt to regain power in an armed rebellion that ultimately proved unsuccessful.

Berry's first meeting was held in the back of a car, since the Russians' offices had been destroyed in the uprising. "I happened to fly in when the buildings were still smoldering," he recalled.

Moscow also faced political upheavals at the time. President Boris Yeltsin dissolved the legislature when the Soviet old guard would not agree to reforms. In response, Soviet supporters rallied in the streets and laid siege to the Russian White House, with lawmakers barricaded inside. Berry recalled the incident:

> During the uprising, the Russian banks couldn't get U.S. dollars, and nobody would send the dollars in because they were frightened. Credit Suisse

phoned me up, although they never used to work with Brink's.

They asked, "Any chance of Brink's getting the dollars into Moscow?"

I contacted a Russian official, who said, "Don't worry. Go ahead and bring it in, and we'll make sure it's delivered."

And that's exactly what I did. ... It was the only dollar shipment for months that got through to Moscow.[11]

According to Alex Borodko, who helped establish Brink's Global Services in Russia in 1995 and now works for Brink's in Ukraine, Brink's presence in Russia came together quickly. "The team, which we created with our partner, was a very good team," he said. "In September 1995, we had the first shipments, and from January to February 1996, we started to develop very fast."

Establishing service in Russia was key, explained Joseph Eyal, because the country has an abundance of gold and platinum mines, and one-third of the world's diamonds. After Wynne found a way to ship banknotes in Russia, Brink's found a way to ship diamonds and quickly became the country's market share leader.[12]

International Innovation

In the early days of Brink's Global Services, shipping processes were highly manual, requiring the frequent use of telex machines, faxes, and telephones. Although not very efficient and subject to manual entry errors, the system provided versatility and quick customization. During the 1990s, Brink's began the highly complex process of creating a global electronic system of communication. "What we do requires high coordination," said Paibul Chanawatr, vice president of information and communication technology for Brink's Global Services Limited. "We were working with customs processes, airports, and customers in 30 to 40 countries. We needed a system that would help everyone speak the same language, use the same forms, and follow the same process—all without giving up the flexibility our customers demanded."

The resulting system was Brink's International Transportation System (BITS). Although the system has evolved significantly since its inception more than 10 years ago and now supports more than 100 countries, the central concept of standardized communication remains the same. "With a global electronic system, we can communicate quickly, accurately, and efficiently," explained Chanawatr. "We enhance the system on an ongoing basis, updating airport regulations and customs changes so that we are always current and delivering the best possible service."

During this time, Brink's innovation was not limited to Brink's Global Services. In 1995, the company introduced Brink's CompuSafe® Service, a combination computer and safe solution marketed toward retail stores, gas stations, and fast-food restaurants. According to Bill Hodnett, vice president of Brink's U.S., the idea for CompuSafe® came about when Meridian Bank in Philadelphia became the first Brink's customer to outsource its back-room currency handling. Hodnett recalled:

We saw the complication and the tedious manual process of what, back in those days, was called envelope processing. In the small retail business, every time a teller got a certain level of cash in the cash register, they pulled it out. They called it an envelope, but they actually just wrapped it with a piece of paper and showed how much it was supposed to be, and they dropped it in a safe,

Gary Landry (left), executive vice president of Brink's International, is shown here with John Connaughton of Brink's, Incorporated. *(Photo courtesy of Brink's Museum.)*

BRINK'S AND ITS TRUCKS

THROUGHOUT THE WORLD, BRINK'S HAS MORE than 9,100 armored vehicles. Each one is special, not only because it carries the corporate brand, but because these trucks protect and support the company's most valuable assets—its people.

Brink's trucks are built by a variety of manufacturers to serve specific purposes. For example, Brink's Brazil custom-designed a truck to withstand the high risk of vehicle attack that is common to that region. Unable to find a truck to meet the region's demanding specifications, Brink's engineering team, along with the fleet department, the chassis manufacturer, and a few of Brink's Brazil's best drivers, convened at the car body designer's plant. There, each party offered input and suggestions. What started as a basic armored truck later emerged with more than 40 modifications.

Weighing more than six tons, the Brink's Brazil truck is a Mercedes Benz 915-E. The 150 hp engine with high torque in both low and high RPMs can carry more than 2.5 tons of cargo. Within the truck, from the floor to the ceiling, the vehicle offers more space and more comfort for truck operators and better thermal efficiency for the crew. State-of-the-art armored technologies protect the occupants from external blasts.

The truck also includes a progressive-concept chassis that combines low fuel consumption with low emission of polluting gases, and has a sleek, contemporary design that enhances the driver's visibility, reduces blind spots, and allows better coordination among crew members in the event of an attack.

Trucks in the Brink's fleet are built by International Harvester, Mercedes Benz, Volkswagen, and other renowned manufacturers.

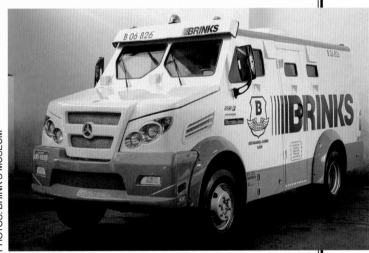

PHOTOS: BRINK'S MUSEUM

just a manual safe. Then counting it was the most labor-intensive work in the back room.[13]

Brink's CompuSafe® Service, a computerized cash-handling system that automatically detects the value of the bills placed in the safe. Once read, the bills were stored in locked cassettes that could only be opened in specialized currency rooms where Brink's employees combined deposits and transferred funds.[14] Bill Gunn, a Brink's employee since 1981, was on the engineering team that designed CompuSafe®.

"We realized that there were many more issues that the stores could solve if we had a little bit more technology, so it evolved fairly quickly," Gunn explained. "CompuSafe® bill accepters have locked cassettes, and as the cashier puts money into the CompuSafe®, it counts the money and stacks it neatly. When Brink's comes, they remove the locked cassettes and replace them with locked empty cassettes, then take the full cassettes back to the Brink's processing center for counting."[15]

The first CompuSafe® customer was a Chevron gas station in Atlanta, Georgia, in 1994. "At that point, we weren't selling to the banks," said Hodnett. "We were selling to the retail customer."

According to Fred Purches, senior vice president of product management and strategic solutions at Brink's U.S.:

CompuSafe® does two things, predominantly. It reduces security risk, in terms of exposure to the public, or potential robbery, and risk in terms of employees stealing money, so you will see where the losses that result in a store go down pretty dramatically when you put one in.

Operationally, people spent a lot of time counting money, whether it was the clerk up front or the store manager at the end of the day preparing a deposit, and all of that goes away for the store [with CompuSafe®].[16]

Violence on the Rise

In the United States, Brink's was feeling the effects of a nationwide rise in bank robberies.[17] "When crime goes up, it's a double-edged sword," said Gary Landry, executive vice president of Brink's International. "Robberies go up, but it also makes security more important to business, and you wind up getting some non-users or some light users using more services."[18]

Brink's armored truck crews faced more danger than they ever had before. "I must share with you both my sadness and concern with the level of violence being experienced in our industry," wrote Brink's Executive Vice President C. Buck Crebs in the Winter 1994 *Brink's Link*. "This year we have

ABOVE AND BEYOND

BRINK'S WORKERS HAVE ALWAYS BEEN KEPT TO A high standard. The company is structured as a "paramilitary" organization, explained John Hague, retired chief financial officer of Brink's U.S. operations. "It garners a certain amount of loyalty that you don't find in other businesses. Frequently, people refer to Brink's the institution … when they talk about the company, and they speak fondly about the institution. Our people do have good feelings about the company in general, and usually, they'll tell you about it."[1]

Courageous Brink's employees have worked day and night to maintain operations during disasters such as hurricanes, earthquakes, and riots.

In 1992, members of the Los Angeles Police Department were acquitted of using excessive force against suspect Rodney King, despite a widely circulated video of the officers beating the suspect. The event triggered a series of vicious riots in South Central Los Angeles, which left more than 50 dead and resulted in almost $1 billion worth of damage. Yet, even in the midst of the chaos and violence of the riots, Brink's continued making its deliveries. According to Gary Landry, executive vice president of Brink's International:

We were right in the middle of it. We had employees who basically abandoned their homes and families to stay at Brink's for five-, six-, and seven-day periods. They would work all day on the street, and then they would post on the rooftop with a shotgun at night with buckets of water and sand as gangs were roving the streets and burning buildings and everything.

the greatest number of shootings in the history of our business."[19]

The surge in violence was also noted in The Pittston Company's 1995 Annual Report, which mentioned that seven guards had been killed that year: "In the past, attacks on Brink's people were relatively rare. Such attacks are now occurring more frequently."[20]

Eleanor Wdovech, executive assistant at Brink's and an employee from 1944 to 1995, said that longtime Brink's employees know that robbery is always a very real possibility. "I never talked about my job to anyone outside the company because it was a self-imposed security rule," said Wdovech. "What if I let slip something that somebody with a criminal mind could use?"[21]

Bill Vecchiarella, Brink's regional vice president of the Great Lake regions, said the focus on employee safety and security was a cultural difference that took some time to adjust to when he left FedEx for Brink's in 1993. "The No. 1 priority at FedEx was to service the customer, and the No. 1 priority at Brink's is to bring our people home safely

every day," said Vecchiarella. "There's a very dangerous element to what we do. It's vitally important that we follow the proven security procedures for everybody's safety."[22]

That sort of concern has always been a hallmark at Brink's, where the shared dangers lead to a strong sense of camaraderie between employees. "I immediately liked the people I worked with and always have," recalled Brad Coles, a longtime Brink's employee who retired in 1996.

Advanced Training

In 1995, with the upsurge in robberies, Brink's decided to upgrade equipment and introduce new company-wide training programs. Dennis Casteel, Brink's director of firearms and training, led the program, which started at the Los Angeles branch in 1996 and expanded to other branches beginning in 2000. The company now has 250 training instructors, including 146 firearms instructors.

"Probably 80 percent of them are all NRA [National Rifle Association] instructors now," said

---

When the arsonists approached Brink's headquarters, they would look up and see 60 or 70 people with shotguns and buckets of sand and water ... and they would turn away and go.

Brink's workers just don't bat an eye in those conditions. They just band together, and they get it done. It's almost like soldiers in a foxhole under fire for 36, 48 hours, with no food and water and no sleep, but if bullets are coming over your head, you get it done.[2]

When Hurricane Katrina struck New Orleans in 2005, 20 employees worked at the city's branch for up to 30 days straight, sleeping in small travel trailers in the parking lot, "sometimes without water and electricity," Landry said. "They would stay there just to be close to the branch to get the job done," delivering cash during the disaster and its aftermath.[3]

Brink's international crews have also been distinguished by their bravery in the line of duty. South African crews, for instance, have been vulnerable to attacks from cars that surround and

sideswipe the armored truck, knocking it over. One particular attack involved seven cars and approximately 30 bandits carrying 200 automatic weapons, said Jane Hamilton, general manager of Brink's South Africa. Although they were vastly outnumbered, she said, "Our crew actually fired at them, fighting back to protect the shipment."

One particularly resilient Brink's employee involved in the incident was shot in the back with an AK-47. "The robbery happened on Thursday, and by the following Tuesday, he was back to work," Hamilton recalled.[4]

In Israel, during the 2006 war with Lebanon, Brink's employees not sent to fight the war worked amid rocket fire. According to Yitzhak Rabin, general manager of Brink's Israel, "We didn't miss one day. Because we say to our employees ... 'Somebody has to provide the money to the ATM machines in order for the people to have money to buy necessities. Otherwise, they will not be able to buy milk or bread.' Our people really understand this."[5]

Casteel, referring to the NRA's certification program for law enforcement firearms instructors.

All Brink's applicants must first pass a standardized 60-round firearms test with at least an 80 percent proficiency rate. Those who do not pass get one more try—if they fail a second time, they cannot work for Brink's.

New hires must complete three days of firearms training with a standard Smith and Wesson 40-caliber pistol, as well as a day-and-a-half orientation class.

"In our program, we have essentially eight different films that we show," said Casteel. "One involves what cover is, and that actually was made by the L.A. County Sheriff's Department. We adopted that. It's a very, very good film. We have a deadly force decisions tape that has different scenarios. We actually have scenarios built into the curriculum, in the book, for discussion, and we have another set of films that actually feature a shoot/don't shoot type of scenario."

Brink's uses a video device that creates virtual scenarios for firearms training. Called a CAPS simulator, "it helps to educate judgment and realistic scenarios," said John Carmichael, Brink's global head of security. "That's a critical factor in making sure that our folks are competent in using their weapons as well as competent in making good decisions about when to use a weapon. We don't want to endanger anyone around us. If something does happen, we want to do everything we can to make sure that our customer's customers are not endangered."

Casteel also led the effort to change the uniforms from the traditional street messenger style with jacket and cap to a more tactical look, with bulletproof vests worn on the outside of the uniform. "I believe that's really helped cut down on robberies," said Casteel. "For years, we had averaged probably 90 attacks industry wide a year, and we saw a big drop probably in 2004, 2005, and 2006."[23]

It's important to be vigilant in updating training programs, said Fred Meitin, retired vice president of security for Brink's Canada. He explained:

These statistics all happen in cycles, and you might get four or five years where you don't have any robberies, and this presents the greatest challenge for the Brink's leadership, which is preventing complacency. Complacency leads to vulnerability and ultimately preventable incidents, and the loss of liability is exceeded only by the loss of life that happens, which cannot be replaced.[24]

International Ventures

In 1997, Brink's launched its biggest start-up yet, in Argentina, with a five-story administra-

Brink's employees in Bolivia practice their firing skills. *(Photo courtesy of Brink's Museum.)*

Above: Since switching from wearing bulletproof vests under the Brink's uniform to wearing them on the outside, where they are visible to would-be criminals, the number of attacks on armed messengers has dropped dramatically.

Below right: Brink's training manuals were customized for each country. Shown is the manual from Brazil. *(Photos courtesy of Brink's Museum.)*

Increasing the volume of Brink's interests in the region proved beneficial because, as Hank Carideo, general manager of Brink's Global Services, explained, "It's a little more expensive to operate because the risk is much higher in most of Latin America."

Also that year, Brink's increased its share from a 15 percent to a 61 percent majority interest in its Venezuelan affiliate Custodia & Traslado De Valores, C.A., the largest armored car company in Venezuela. A group of Venezuelan banks held the remaining 39 percent. The Venezuelan affiliate also owned a 31 percent interest in Brink's Peru, S.A.[26]

Meanwhile, Brink's continued its buyout of its European partnerships. The company acquired the remaining 35 percent of its Netherlands affiliate, Brink's Nedlloyd, for $2 million plus an additional payment tied to profits gained within the next two years.[27] It expanded its presence in Switzerland with a partnership with Swiss freight handling company Zürcher Freilager (ZF). Brink's owned 51 percent of the resulting joint venture. ZF provided freight-handling, vaulting, and ware-

tive building, three vaults, and 25 trucks serving Buenos Aires and 13 other cities.

"Establishing a presence in Argentina gave Brink's representation in eight of the 13 countries on the South American mainland, in a nation with one of the most stable economies in the world today, an annual inflation rate of less than 2 percent and the peso pegged at parity with the U.S. dollar," read an article in *Brink's Link Worldwide*. Naldo Dasso, a former general and second-in-command in the Argentine army, ran the company's security department.[25]

In 1997, Brink's once again took majority ownership in its Venezuelan operations. *(Photo courtesy of Brink's Museum.)*

housing services, while Brink's supplied management expertise and technology.[28]

With new partners in Switzerland, Brink's revenues there grew 20 percent to 25 percent. "We worked hard to get relationships with the banks, and we were able to get close to the refineries and started to do lots of metals and banknotes business in and out of Switzerland," said Vice President Dominik Bossart, who worked for Brink's in Switzerland at the time.

In 1998, at a cost of $39 million, Brink's purchased the remaining 62 percent of shares of Brink's S.A.—the largest armored car company in France at the time and Brink's largest European affiliate.[29] The acquisition included Brink's French subsidiaries in Côte d'Ivoire, French Guiana, and the French West Indies, and Île de Réunion in the Indian Ocean near East Africa.[30]

Christian Berté, former chief financial officer of Brink's France and future chief financial officer of Brink's EMEA in Paris, admitted that, at the time, the French organization, faced "a significant challenge in terms of organization of finances," and was in need of reorganizing and restructuring. "That was the primary goal and reason why I joined the organization—because of the challenge they were giving me to help the company to do better in a specific field of organization."[31]

In 1998, Brink's acquired the remaining 50 percent of Brink's-Schenker GmbH, its German operation, for $3 million. It renamed the affiliate Brink's Deutschland GmbH.[32] The German affiliate had been launched in 1972 as a partnership between Brink's-MAT in the United Kingdom and a subsidiary of the nationalized West German railroad system. When Germany was reunified in 1990, German freight conglomerate Stinnes, AG, became a Brink's partner.[33]

License to Grow

The Brink's name opens a lot of doors, according to Tracy Heiner, vice president of sales for Brink's U.S. "We always get a ticket. We don't always get to play, but we always get a ticket because of our branding, and that is a wonderful thing when you're in the sales ranks and you're out there, and you're pounding the streets, and you're trying to overcome the objections that are out there."[34]

To expand services and further profit from its brand name with licensing agreements, Brink's began actively seeking partnerships with other companies. In 1998, Brink's Home Security (BHS) licensed its name to Sisco, Inc., for a line of home safes sold in retail stores to compete with Sentry, the No. 1 safe manufacturer.[35] Over the next few years, BHS would enter a number of such licensing agreements with recognized brands to further expand the company's name recognition and market share.

During this time, BHS partnered with DirecTV to market, sell, and install the satellite television service to BHS customers.[36]

Big Bank Ideas

While keeping step with banking technology, Brink's also had to adapt to changes in the U.S. banking industry. The Supreme Court had declared interstate banking constitutional in the 1980s, paving the way for successful banks to grow larger and buy up smaller local banks around the country. The fact that these large banks wanted consistency in Brink's services from state to state led Brink's to rethink its decentralization approach, which allowed branch managers relative autonomy as long as things ran smoothly. Shellie Crandall, senior vice president of Brink's U.S., described the transition:

GOING GLOBAL WITH BRINK'S GLOBAL SERVICES

BRINK'S EXTENSIVE WORLDWIDE PRESENCE IS DUE, in large part, to the growth of Brink's Global Services (BGS). This division specializes in managing risk through the safe, secure transportation and handling of valuables, including diamonds, jewelry, precious metals, securities, currency, high-tech devices, and more, from packing and pickup through inventory control to final delivery.

Officially formed in 1998 by the merger of Brink's Air Courier and Brink's Diamond and Jewelry, BGS today serves more than 110 countries through an integrated network of 900 offices on six continents.

"Brink's Global Services helped us complete the transformation from a U.S.-based company with international operations to a truly global enterprise," said Joseph Eyal. "We continue to evolve, developing the solutions and services companies need to succeed in today's increasingly global economy."

BGS leverages state-of-the-art proprietary information and communication systems and a varied array of secure transportation methods, including armored trucks and trailers, secure air and sea freight, air charters (fixed wing and helicopters), and couriers and armed messengers, to safeguard and transport some of the world's most valuable assets. BGS serves companies from many industries, including airlines and airports, financial institutions, governments, mines, diamonds and jewelry, high-tech, pharmaceutical, precious metals, and information technology, to name a few.

Key services:

- Secure transportation
- Trade show services
- Cash processing
- Customs clearance services
- Inventory management
- Walk-in service centers
- Secure Data Solutions
- Consultancy services

The company realized we needed to not be so decentralized ... so that our services were more standard across the U.S. footprint, without ruining that autonomy at the lowest level. I can't possibly make all the decisions, and I wouldn't make them right, versus the manager that's on the ground there at the local level saying, "Hey, I need to do this and I need to do that."[37]

Greg Hanno, senior vice president of human resources for Brink's U.S., recalled some "big, pretty complicated" organizational changes that came in 1999: "The company had drifted into a structure of 24 general managers who basically had an awful lot of independence and autonomy and were pretty much running what looked like independent businesses."

Management was consolidated from 24 to nine regions in 1999. "We put some resources on the regional team to support the branches and then drive some consistency from one region to the next," Hanno said.[38]

With a streamlined management team in the United States, a strong and growing global network, and a host of industry-related innovations to its credit, Brink's stood ready for its next challenge. In the 2000s, the company would make the crucial shift to The Brink's Company, selling off the underperforming assets of The Pittston Company to focus on armed transport, security, technological advances, and international expansion.

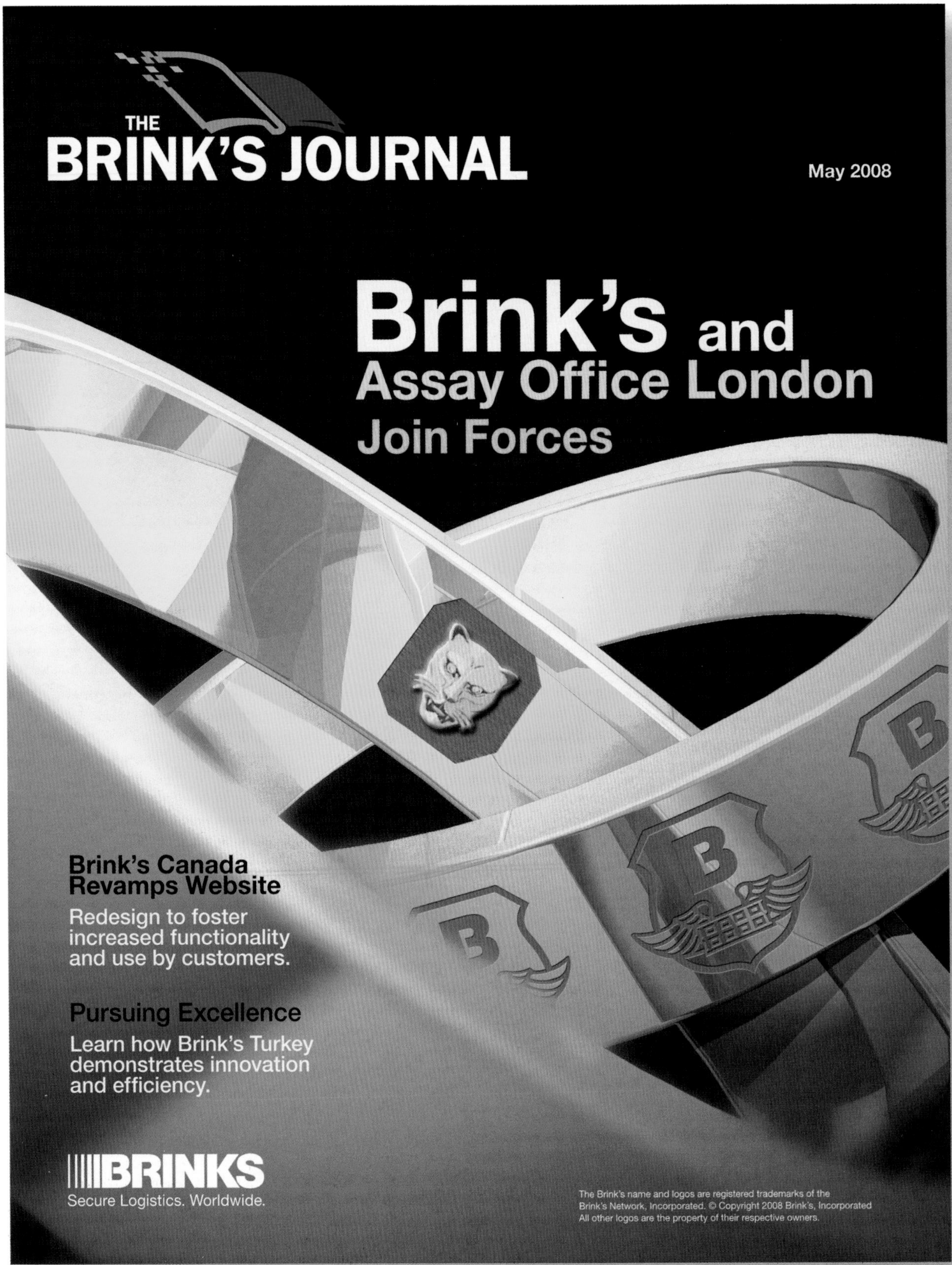

THE
BRINK'S JOURNAL
May 2008
Brink's and
Assay Office London
Join Forces
Brink's Canada
Revamps Website
Redesign to foster
increased functionality
and use by customers.
Pursuing Excellence
Learn how Brink's Turkey
demonstrates innovation
and efficiency.
BRINKS
Secure Logistics. Worldwide.
The Brink's name and logos are registered trademarks of the
Brink's Network, Incorporated. © Copyright 2008 Brink's, Incorporated
All other logos are the property of their respective owners.

Brink's and Assay Office London joined forces in 2008 to offer customers a premier hallmarking facility with the secure premises of Brink's Global Services at Heathrow Airport.

CHAPTER TEN

A BRAND-NEW BRINK'S

2001–PRESENT

Security is everything to us.

—Jim Spurlock, vice president of employee relations[1]

BRINK'S ASSISTANT MANAGER BOB Barrett was sitting at his desk at the Brooklyn, New York, branch on September 11, 2001, when he heard on the radio that a plane had hit the World Trade Center. He immediately alerted his boss. About 15 minutes later, the second plane hit, and it soon became obvious that the two incidents held deeper implications. Terrorists had attacked the United States.

"I started to think, 'Oh, my God, what's happening here?'" Barrett said.[2]

In response, the manager of the armored car division called back all trucks on duty in New York City and the surrounding New Jersey area. Barrett recalled the fear after the attacks:

We wanted to get all the trucks back to our Brooklyn base as fast as possible. In plain English, nobody knew what the hell was going on.

As a safety precaution, the Brooklyn building was surrounded with our armored cars. We put up 80 men on the roof of the building with their rifles and pistols and shotguns just for security. We lined the roof of the building like an army, and in the parking lot and around the building, we had everything bumper to bumper. You got in by somebody backing the trucks up. It was a pretty tense time.[3]

After the attacks, the Federal Aviation Administration grounded all civilian aircraft in the United States and Canada. "We had planes that we were expecting to land at Miami International Airport after they'd closed all the airports," said Brink's Global Services' Jenny Cole, who focused on the Latin American region and worked out of Miami, Florida, at the time. "Those planes had to be diverted—planes with millions and millions of dollars on board."[4]

Across the globe, banks awaiting deliveries or pickups faced delays as Brink's rushed to bring order to the chaos. According to Cole:

We had to say fairly quickly, "We were expecting to take this money back from you, but now we're not going to be able to. Can we house it in your central bank?"

I had one situation in the Caymans where we had picked up from a number of locations. Ordinarily, we would have just flown it out, but the plane was turned back after it had taken off out of the Caymans. We had to recover all of the currency off that flight, and then make arrangements with

---

After the company's success in Hong Kong, Brink's expanded to the Macau region of mainland China.

Brink's workers were on the scene in the aftermath of the 2001 World Trade Center attacks. *(Photo courtesy of Brink's Museum.)*

the central bank in the Grand Caymans to vault the money for the time being.[5]

At the time of the attacks, Brink's Guard Joe Trombino had been in the middle of a delivery in the basement of the World Trade Center. He was one of nearly 3,000 people killed in the attacks. A Korean War veteran, the 68-year-old had planned to retire in a year, his wife, Jean, told the *New York Times.* "He'd done that for so long, it was like he didn't know what else to do," she said.[6]

Coal Closure

In 2002, Brink's parent company, The Pittston Company, announced plans to sell off its costly natural resource holdings, which had increasingly become an antiquated liability. "Coal was an awful business," noted a *Barron's* article on Brink's. "If you looked at it over time, it never earned its cost of capital."[7]

2001
Brink's Guard Joe Trombino is killed in the September 11 attacks on the World Trade Center. He had been in the middle of making a delivery when the first plane struck.

BRINK'S MUSEUM

2003
The Pittston Company becomes The Brink's Company.

BRINK'S MUSEUM

|||PITTSTON

2002
Pittston, Brink's parent company, announces plans to sell off its natural resource holdings.

More than a decade of attempts at restructuring Pittston had taken its toll. According to the article, "Brink's is neither widely followed nor particularly well-loved on Wall Street. ... The Richmond, Virginia–based company simply doesn't fit tidily into one industry."

Lacking a clear focus, the company had sales of $4 billion annually, but was worth only $1 billion to shareholders.[8] Executives decided to take action. In 2002, Pittston's coal interests were sold to Virginia-based Massey Energy Company and Connecticut-based First Reserve Corporation.[9] Additional mines were sold in November 2003 to Appalachian Fuels, LLC, for approximately $14 million.[10]

The sale, said Jack T. Walsh, retired executive vice president, "was very strategic in allowing us to concentrate on our core business."

Increasingly unburdened by Pittston's coal interests, 88 percent of shareholders voted to change the company's name from Pittston to The Brink's Company, with BCO as the new stock symbol.

In 2000, Brink's trucks were used in promotional material for the New York Lottery and for Harry Winston's transport of the 41-carat Dresden Green Diamond, second only to the Hope Diamond in rarity and uniqueness. *(Photo courtesy of George Kanatous.)*

2006

BAX Global is sold.

BRINK'S MUSEUM

2004

Brink's Document Destruction Service is launched.

BRINK'S MUSEUM

2008

Brink's Home Security is spun off from Brink's as a separate corporation.

A FALLEN HERO

JOSEPH TROMBINO, A LONGTIME Brink's guard, survived the Weather Underground robbery in 1981 despite being shot multiple times by an M16 rifle. It took three operations to sew his nearly severed arm back on.[1]

On the morning of September 11, 2001, Trombino was part of a three-person crew making a delivery to the World Trade Center. According to John Muhlenforth, Brink's operations manager in Brooklyn, New York, and a personal friend of Trombino:

> Every day, they would go into the World Trade Center, pull down into the loading bay area, and back in against the loading platform near the Port Authority police station. There was a station down below. They would off-load their delivery for the Bank of America and then go on the freight elevator, and go up to the 11th floor and drop it off, with Joe remaining in the front compartment of the vehicle.[2]

While his coworkers headed upstairs, Trombino guarded the truck and its cargo and received packages for other crews also making Bank of America deliveries. After the first plane hit the World Trade Center, Muhlenforth said, "Joe called the base to see what was going on. He was told to leave the vehicle and exit the building ASAP."

Trombino's partner, Nigel Linton, recalled the day starting off like any other day. "We told Joe to stay in the truck because he was an older guy," said Linton. "We had three young guys. If something happens up there, it's better for us to be there."

On May 5, 2003, Chairman and CEO Michael Dan celebrated the change by ringing the opening bell on the New York Stock Exchange. "The firm hopes the name change will highlight Brink's exit from the coal business," noted an article on the event in the *Richmond Times-Dispatch* of Virginia.[11]

In August 2003, Brink's sold its natural gas operations to an affiliate of First Reserve Corporation for approximately $81 million. Of that, $50 million went directly into the Voluntary Employees' Beneficiary Association, a legacy fund designed to cover health liabilities for former Pittston miners. Brink's maintained a $742 million obligation on the fund and planned to add up to $100 million from the sale of its natural resource interests.

Wall Street responded positively to the sale, and Brink's stock rose from $14 to more than $20 per share.[12]

"Anything that moves [Brink's] away from the coal and gas industry is a big plus," said investment banker Jack Mallon in the *Daily Deal* newspaper. "It's been an overhanging cloud on their organization."[13]

Just two original Pittston assets remained. In December 2003, Brink's closed a $38 million deal to sell its timber operations to Forestland Group of Chapel Hill, North Carolina, a timberland investment man-

Waiting to pick up a delivery, they stopped at the restroom on their way to the 44ᵗʰ floor. Then the first plane struck the tower.

"The whole building shook, and then we heard a loud explosion," recalled Joseph Gebhardt, a Brink's guard who survived the attack. "We thought it was a bomb or something. When we opened the door, there was smoke all over."

They tried to head back to the Bank of America offices, but smoke and debris blocked their way. They then tried the stairs, which were already crowded with frightened people making their way down. Struggling down 14 flights took 10 minutes. By the time they neared the first floor, Linton said, "people were screaming, 'The door is stuck! Go back upstairs!'"

However, they continued pressing forward, and the door eventually came unglued.

"It was like a war zone," said Linton. "The whole first floor was blown out. The whole lobby was gone. I passed a lady who was burnt from head to toe. I looked out on the street. All of it was paper and debris."

Trombino, meanwhile, was still in the basement. According to Muhlenforth, Trombino refused to leave without first grabbing the truck's cargo:

He grabbed the cargo, which contained ... boxes of jewelry and so on, some securities, and he left the building. But I guess due to the trauma that was going on and the disarray of where he was going, he was trapped between the North Tower and the South Tower where the water fountain would have been in the circle. He lost consciousness, and after the attack, his lifeless body was found there.[3]

"We lost a real nice guy," said Brink's Assistant Manager Bob Barrett, who still cannot bring himself to watch footage of the attacks. "I think he was a 35- or 40-year Brink's man, only a year or so away from retirement."

As the day progressed, many of the Brooklyn workers were sent home early.

"A lot of them have family, children," Barrett continued. "They were worried. It was pretty traumatic, and then, of course, we heard that we lost one of our own. It hurt. It hurt. As you know, the whole nation, the city, was pretty much in shock."[4]

agement firm.[14] Later that year, Brink's also sold a gold mine in Australia to MPI Mines, Limited, for approximately $27 million.[15]

BAX Brings in a Bundle

With the natural gas, coal, and timber resources sold off, Brink's executives began to focus on selling Burlington Air Express (BAX). Revenues at BAX began faltering in 1997 due to a decline in heavy freight shipped overnight in the United States, which offset any profits Brink's showed on its balance sheet.[16]

"It created a lot of pressure on Brink's over the years because we had to make up the difference," said Gary Landry, regarding BAX. "The industry was volatile, and as a result the company was volatile. Analysts would get frustrated, and Wall Street would get very frustrated with us as an orga-nization because of the volatility of that. There was always a lot of pressure."[17]

Internationally, however, BAX consistently turned a profit. Fixed costs remained lower abroad, since BAX could more easily rent space on commercial carriers during overnight international flights. The U.S. operation, on the other hand, had to purchase and maintain its own planes.[18]

In 2003, Brink's board of directors and shareholders began pressuring Dan to sell BAX. However, BAX had recently been showing signs of recovery, and Dan wanted to wait a few years to see if the company could sell at a higher price. "We were making money for the first time," he recalled. "The competition was on the ropes."[19]

By early 2004, BAX "showed strong profit gains as the Americas returned to profitability," according to a Brink's press release.[20] Dan added:

BAX kept getting better and better and better. I told the board, "I can sell this for $750 million."

The investment banker said, "You'd be lucky to get $300 million."

Wall Street analysts speculated the sale could bring in $600 million.[21]

The market responded positively when Brink's announced it was seeking a buyer for BAX; the company's share price jumped 13.5 percent. In the end, Dan proved they had all underestimated the value of BAX. In November 2005, Dan announced that Deutsche Bahn, the German national railway company, had agreed to purchase Burlington Air Express for $1.1 billion.[22]

BAX and Deutsche Bahn had "an amazing footprint overlap," said Frank Lennon, Brink's vice president and chief administrative officer.

On May 5, 2003, Chairman and CEO Michael Dan (sixth from right) celebrated the name change from The Pittston Company to The Brink's Company by ringing the opening bell on the New York Stock Exchange. *(Photo courtesy of Brink's Museum.)*

"Deutsche Bahn had a relatively small operation in the States where BAX Global was really dominant in the heavy cargo market, and they had a fantastic array outside of the United States. And in many instances, they were dominant in areas where BAX was not dominant. So the fit was almost hand in glove."[23]

The sale closed in January 2006. Approximately $600 million of the proceeds went toward repurchasing 20 percent of outstanding Brink's shares, and $200 million went toward paying down other outstanding debt.[24]

Brink's used an additional $200 million to pay down the company's debt toward paying healthcare costs for retired coal miners—liability the company carried over from the Pittston days.

"The stock prices obviously started to take off because the liabilities were resolved for the first time," said Dan. "We were a much simpler company. Just a security company."[25]

More Than Armored Trucks

Even without the coal mining assets and BAX, Brink's is more than armored trucks. Across the

No One Has Ever Lost a Penny

BRINK'S PROUD MOTTO, "NO ONE HAS EVER LOST a penny entrusting their valuables to Brink's" is more than a testament to the company's security and risk management expertise. It is also proof of the company's fiscal responsibility and sound business practices.

Armored transportation company shipments are usually covered by industry-specific insurance. Exclusions, premiums, payouts, and coverages are determined by the strength and stability of the armored transportation company. Insurers seek to mitigate their risk by imposing on the transportation company strict operating guidelines, any infraction of which could invalidate coverage and expose the provider—and its customers—to losses. Secure logistics providers with top-tier financial strength are rarely subject to insurance-mandated operating guidelines and, as a result, claims are not likely to be denied based on noncompliance.

Brink's takes this one step further, with the financial wherewithal to pay claims out-of-pocket. In fact, Brink's often chooses to settle with customers first to avoid delay, dealing with the insurance company later for its own reimbursement.

Although Brink's carries industry-leading insurance, the company operates as a self-regulated provider, unencumbered by insurance audits and free to enforce its own guidelines in accordance with business and customer objectives.

globe, Brink's lends its signature brand of trust to a diverse array of risk management services designed to protect customers and their most valuable assets.

In Latin America, this diversity can be seen in the form of a walk-in bill payment and collections service called Brink's ePago International. Acquired in 2006, ePago allows billers (banks, retailers, and utilities) to optimize their customer service payment centers by moving from collecting only one monthly bill to accepting a multitude of bills at the same location, thereby increasing the volume of transactions per location. Adding Brink's ePago International has been a powerful play in Latin America in moving Brink's toward integrated technology solutions along with the company's core expertise in secure cash logistics. Brink's ePago International's General Manager Ricardo Ramírez explained, "What we convey to our customers—banks, retailers, etcetera—is that while the technology behind ePago is core to our value proposition, the real differentiator is the high level of service we provide to their customers."

In Europe, Brink's guarding services play an increasing critical role in reinforcing the company's trust and market leadership. Recently, the U.S. government took an important step in protecting its diplomatic missions in Greece by awarding a five-year contract to Brink's Hellas. Under this agreement, Brink's provides security services, including entry control, visitor screenings with portable and fixed metal detectors, X-ray package screening, roving patrols, and security control center operations. Brink's security operations in the Netherlands and Germany were awarded similar diplomatic contracts for their work with the U.S. embassies in those nations.

Using the company's network of armored trucks and secure vault facilities, Brink's Secure Data Solutions is an example of leveraging existing expertise to fulfill an emerging need. In the early 2000s, several large companies suffered high profile losses and public disgrace when they lost computer tapes containing the names, social security numbers, and account data of thousands of unsuspecting customers. Brink's was the first secure transportation company to venture into the world of data security and continues to lead the market in secure transportation and storage of backup data tapes and other sensitive media.

Throughout the world, the Brink's brand of trust is also stamped on airports, where security teams are called upon to inspect passengers at check-in and boarding, control aircraft access and restricted areas, inspect baggage, and control airport freight. In fact, in France, Brink's is one of the few companies authorized by the Ministry of Transport to validate companies that ship freight and deliver products directly on airplanes.

Global Changes Keep Things Moving

Ever mindful of new international opportunities, Brink's expanded its operations in Luxembourg and Dubai and shifted its focus in the United Kingdom. It also turned around flagging operations in Australia and Argentina.

"Brink's, as an organization, is very cautious," observed Ian Nunn, Brink's U.S. chief financial officer. "At the same time, there are plenty of seeds that are planted, such as the company's representative office in Moscow, which has been there for 10 years."[26]

In Luxembourg, Brink's small operation employed a staff of 41 until the company acquired competitor Securicor in 2005. Founded as a security services firm in 1972, Securicor expanded in the late 1970s to include technical security services and alarm installation and monitoring. In 1985, it ventured into the money-transport business.[27] In 2004, in order to merge with security firm Group 4 Falck, it had to divest of competing operations under the terms of the European Commission.[28]

The purchase raised Brink's profile considerably in Luxembourg. "Securicor was a company with around a thousand people," said Carlo Weisen, managing director of Brink's Luxembourg. "It was a very profitable business, and it still is a very profitable business."[29]

Brink's also increased its Middle Eastern operations in 2005, adding a new branch at the Dubai Metals and Commodities Centre offering services to the rapidly expanding gold and diamond industry.[30]

In the United Kingdom, Brink's sold its flagging domestic cash transportation service operations to competitor Loomis UK Limited in 2007. Profits had been down in prior years, according to Brink's CEO Michael Dan, because of "competitive pricing pressures, changing regulatory and labor issues, and higher security threats."[31]

Today, Brink's UK operations are among the company's most profitable and the most successful. Home to one of the leading cash centers in the world, Brink's UK continues to bring fresh and innovative solutions to a mature market. According to Dan, "Brink's remains committed to the UK, but taking action to eliminate the negative financial impact was the right thing to do."

In Argentina, Brink's had been losing money every year since it began operations in 1997. Gabriel Allen, CEO of Brink's Argentina, arrived from PepsiCo in 2002 to turn things around. His strategy involved hiring a specialized professional team and developing new niches in the market, such as its CompuSafe® and Secure Logistics services for transporting high-value items, including pharmaceuticals and electronics.

"We developed a program that we named High Performance Team," said Allen. "It's like continuous improvement for all the people here in the company.

Gabriel Allen, CEO of Brink's Argentina, poses in front of a Brink's Argentina truck.

WALKIE-TALKIE MEN

BRINK'S FOCUS ON SECURITY HAS BEEN THE DRIVING force in numerous innovations throughout the years, many of which became the industry standard for armored transportation companies throughout the world.

In addition to the now-famous Two-Key Safe, Brink's also developed the first messenger communication system. Using a one-way radio manufactured by Motorola, the communication system allowed the driver of an armored car to hear his partner while on the street. The communication system, called the Pocket Transmitter, evolved into the modern-day walkie-talkie and marked the start of the company's deep-seated drive to create the industry's most advanced global communication systems.

My objective was to be better day-by-day. Not only 10 percent or 15 percent a year. I want to be better day-by-day, if it's 1 percent in each area."[32]

Once a month, Allen would choose a route and dress for work in a guard's uniform. "I went into the truck, and I did the route with all the crew," he said.

The strategy helped him understand how the business worked from the ground up, he said. It also helped Brink's customer relations. "When I presented myself to one customer, they were very impressed," said Allen. "'How is a CEO, in some cases, working as a guard?'"[33]

Brink's executives in Canada follow a similar approach that has been fundamental to the region's success. "Four times a year, we put on a uniform," said Larry Rodo, executive vice president of Brink's North America. "We put on a firearm and go out to spend eight or nine hours driving a truck, being a guard, being a messenger, working in the money room, or just doing whatever we have to do. At the end of the day, we debrief with the local management. This is what we learned. This is what we found. We sat with your employees for eight hours. You know what? You can't fake it for eight hours. You may be pleasant for an hour, but after eight hours of being together, you learn a lot about what's going on."

After a long process of negotiations, in 2009 Brink's Global Services struck a deal with the Brink's subcontractor in Russia to create the new Brink's operating entity in Russia. This development, which underscores Brink's commitment to enhance its global footprint continually, allows Brink's to provide a variety of services in the country, including international and domestic global services, Cash in Transit, ATM, and security services.

21st-Century Security

Brink's global expansion brought the company face-to-face with some of the world's toughest criminals—aggressive criminals with access to state-of-the-art weapons and explosives more powerful than those that may be used legally by an armored truck driver.

Since the early 2000s, Brink's has been developing security innovations and programs designed to deter theft, minimize the losses, and reduce the risks associated with criminal activity. These innovations play an increasingly important role in Brink's global operations, particularly in countries where Brink's employees are prohibited legally from carrying weapons in the course of their workday.

Such is the case in Belgium. At one time considered one of Brink's most dangerous locations, the company's Belgium operations are now among the safest, thanks in large part to a sophisticated smoke box process. Smoke boxes, which are widely used in countries where Brink's employees are unable to carry guns, are used to transport cash. The boxes are armed with a mechanism that, when detonated, releases thick smoke, staining the cash and anything that touches it and making a robber easy to spot—often "red-handed."

In Belgium, every currency order is packed in its own individual smoke box and armed. These smoke boxes are loaded onto trucks with racks specially designed to accommodate them. When a smoke box is removed from the rack, it is activated and ready to detonate automatically if it does not make contact with a sensor located at the customer premise within a specified period of time.

"Our trucks are clearly marked to let criminals know there is no sense in attacking," says Gary Taylor, Brink's senior vice president of international operations. "The number of attacks on Brink's messengers has decreased dramatically. In Belgium, we have not had any attacks since this technology was put in place."

Brink's France has spearheaded another state-of-the-art security technology designed to protect employees and deter criminal activity: voice analyzers. Leveraging advanced military technology, these devices detect levels of stress in an employee's voice, allowing workers in remote monitoring locations to step in and help—before the threat escalates.

"We can shut down access to the vault from a remote location or activate an ATM kiosk or a smoke machine that dispenses smoke so thick it would be impossible for the perpetrator to see anything," says Taylor.

Remote access technology has also proved invaluable to ATM security in Brink's operations around the world. Special keys fitted with infrared chips sense when a messenger is in close proximity to the designated ATM and provides access accordingly. If a messenger were to approach an ATM out of sequence or tried to open a machine that is not in the specified route, access would be denied.

Partnering Up

During the past eight years, Brink's has continued its strategy of partnering with firms that offered cutting-edge technology in an effort to remain current with its customers' increasingly complex electronic banking and security needs.

Brink's initiated a commercial, on-site document shredding service in 2004, featuring a fleet of mobile shredding vehicles, "capable of destroying in 15 minutes what would take days using older processes," according to a company press release. Most of the workers in this division had previously worked as Brink's guards and were experienced at handling sensitive information, giving the company an edge over competing firms.[34]

As the delivery and processing of paper checks became increasingly handled through electronic means, Brink's entered the check-imaging business in 2007. It focused on scanning checks at its own remote vaults, freeing up bank employees.[35] Remote imaging also sped up the check-clearing process. Brink's partnered in the venture with bank technology firm Metavante.[36]

Identity theft also became an increasing concern for businesses in the United States after several well-publicized incidents involving stolen data from discarded computer equipment, including sensitive information such as social security and credit card numbers. Brink's recognized a growing market for data security and launched Secure Data Solutions in 2005, specializing in protecting, transporting, and destroying sensitive company data on computer tapes and other offline media.[37]

In 2007, Brink's formed partnerships with banks and other suppliers to make better use of new technology. The company announced plans to introduce iDeposit, an online deposit ticket scanned at Brink's facilities that would allow retailers' accounts to be credited the same day. Brink's also developed CompuSafe® 4000, a high-powered safe with two vending-machine–style bill acceptors that could read, count, and stack up to 150 bills at a time. It was also designed to improve security and speed deposit credits for supermarkets and other high-volume retailers.[38]

Divestiture of BHS

Attention turned to Brink's Home Security (BHS) as several top investors issued filings with the Securities and Exchange Commission (SEC) calling for the parent company to spin off or sell the division. They also pushed for representation on Brink's board of directors.

In 2004, top minority shareholders in Brink's began calling for the company to either sell off BHS or spin it off into a separate company. Two hedge fund operators went as far as calling for such action in SEC filings. Despite the intense pressure, Brink's took a conservative approach, considering all of its options over a protracted period of time before making a decision.[39]

BRINK'S AND TECHNOLOGY

FROM ITS EARLY EMBRACE OF THE AUTOMOBILE IN 1904 to its implementation of on-site payroll check-cashing services in the 1920s, Brink's ability to predict and adapt to evolving technology has proved key to the company's success. "I've been getting the *Brink's Link* and noticed how Brink's has changed over the years," said Joe Hasselhoff, who retired as vice president of the southeast region in 1985. "They've really evolved into a technology-driven company in the years since I left."

One of the ways Brink's stays on top of emerging technology trends is through its on-staff engineering department, the only one of its kind in the industry. "Our engineering department is the heart of our R&D efforts," said Guy Weissberg, executive vice president of global logistics. "This team helps us stay in front of the curve and leverage new technologies to meet our customers' increasingly complex secure logistics needs."[1]

Adapting to emerging technologies and changing cus-

tomer needs is likely to remain a substantial focus of Brink's future growth strategy, noted Jim Poteet, senior vice president of product management and development for Brink's U.S. He added:

Long term, we want to get to the point where our new product lines are generating 5 percent of our growth year over year, with organic growth within our core business lines also generating 5 percent year over year, so we continue to grow at 10 percent or greater.[2]

Fred Purches, senior vice president of product management and strategic solutions for Brink's U.S., concurred:

Innovation is our nature; it is part of who we are as an organization. We have never been a company to rest on its laurels. Our success comes from coming up with new things and finding new ways to help our customers be successful at what they do.[3]

BRINK'S MUSEUM

MMI Investments, in a 2006 SEC filing, advised Brink's to split up or consider a leveraged buyout, recapitalization, or self-tender.[40]

In 2008, after much deliberation, the board of directors reached a decision to spin off BHS into a separate, stand-alone company with its own board, staff, and stock listing.

Brink's announced in February 2008 that it would spin off BHS. The process was scheduled for completion in late 2008, with shareholders expected to hold shares of two stand-alone publicly traded companies in a tax-free stock distribution. In a memo to Brink's employees, Michael Dan noted that the spin-off "concludes a very thorough strategic review process."[41]

Tomorrow's Technology Today

Since the early days of Brink's, when the company became one of the first in Chicago to own a telephone, technology and innovation have been woven into the fabric of Brink's culture. For more than 15 decades, Brink's has pushed innovation to its limits, investing capital to support a state-of-the-art technology infrastructure and a full-time engineering department—the only one of its kind—dedicated to driving new and creative solutions to both current and anticipated risk management challenges.

In Belgium, for example, the 21st century has brought Brink's into the age of robotics. Here, where more than 100,000 pensioners receive their payments in the form of cash, Brink's automatic systems use mechanical arms to put together packages of euro notes and coins, first picking out the notes and then opening the plastic envelope with a puff of air, inserting the currency into the plastic envelope, affixing a label with the pensioner's name, and putting the packages in boxes to go to the post office for distribution.

"Manually, it took 30 people working three shifts to get the job done," said Gary Taylor, Brink's senior vice president of international operations. "All of that has been replaced with one robotics system that is faster, more accurate, and more secure than any human process could be."

The Internet also plays an important role in Brink's technology solutions. Brink's customers can monitor their cash position, place change orders, submit deposits, and research discrepancies through Brink's Web-based information tools. Similarly, Brink's Global Services (BGS) customers can monitor shipments through a service called AirClic. This unique program operates on a cellular phone with an attached scanner, serving as a track-and-trace solution for BGS shipments by capturing specific information at certain transfer points to deliver visibility, accountability, and operations efficiency via the World Wide Web.

Brink's U.S. was the first location to introduce check-imaging solutions, a sophisticated service that enables electronic check presentment at remote locations, facilitating faster clearing, reducing risk, and helping bank customers expand their reach beyond their brick-and-mortar networks.

Although officially launched in the 1990s, Brink's CompuSafe® Service also received a boost from 21st-century technology. Later-model safes are equipped with wireless communication technology that facilitates Brink's Daily Credit, a specialized service that gives customers credit for their deposits, based on electronically reported totals, long before the cash is picked up and taken to a Brink's facility for processing. In 2008, the company introduced

another industry first—a Brink's CompuSafe® with integrated check imaging.

"Combining check-imaging capabilities with our CompuSafe® solution was the next logical step forward in creating a robust payment management solution for retailers," said Fred Purches, senior vice president of strategic solutions and product development for Brink's U.S. "This is another example of our technology leadership and our commitment to helping retailers take advantage of new efficiencies and cost savings."

Throughout the Brink's network, cash and coin processing is driven by advanced technology. Brinks' Supersorters, for example, are the company's proprietary coin sorting and counting equipment that deliver the highest throughput speed in the industry. The billions of coins that pass through these extraordinary machines are then enveloped in transparent, split-proof plastic wrap created by Brink's for greater convenience and superior security. Brink's currency processing also leverages the industry's most sophisticated technology to count, sort, and verify more than

In 2007, Brink's released new versions of its popular CompuSafe®, including the CompuSafe® 4000, which is capable of counting up to 16 bills per second. *(Photo courtesy of Brink's Museum.)*

140 types of notes, from the Australian dollar to the Polish zloty.

In London, for instance, Brink's operates multiple cash centers, three of which have been developed to meet the unique needs and requirements of specific customers. In one of these centers, Brink's manages foreign currency operations for a large financial institution, leveraging proprietary equipment and specially designed communications software to count, sort, and verify currencies into denomination-specific packets. Then, borrowing technology from the food-packaging industry, the cash center sends the packets of currency along a conveyor belt where they are shrink-wrapped and packaged according to the needs of each of the 1,600 locations to which the cash is shipped via armored courier.

"Hand-picking and packaging this volume of currencies was laborious and subject to human error," said Orit Eyal-Fibeesh, managing director of Brink's Limited. "This completely automated solution not only speeds processing and ensures both security and accuracy throughout the entire operation, it also allows us to help our customer deliver industry-leading service to their customers."

"Brink's commitment to technology is not selective," says Roger Santone, Brink's senior vice president of information technology. "If there is technology that can make a process more secure, more efficient, or more cost-effective, Brink's is the first to take a look at how it might be incorporated into its business operations."

Unique Solutions

Working closely with customers to create the ideal solution is a Brink's trademark. "Off-the-shelf solutions may work for some companies, but we've always believed that it is our customers' unique needs that drive true innovation," said Brink's president and CEO Michael Dan. "We approach challenges with an open mind. Instead of matching our products to the customer's need, we ask ourselves how we can best help our customers succeed. It may sound like semantics, but this difference, I believe, makes all the difference in the world."

An example of this approach can be seen in Brink's relationship with Christian Dior, the global luxury brand that produces jewelry, handbags,

shoes, fashion accessories, and other merchandise. Through collaboration with the customer, Brink's France expanded its risk management capabilities via a state-of-the-art, full-service distribution center to meet Dior's specifications on packaging, picking up, transporting, and storing its luxury goods. From controls and verifications to stock management and reporting, Brink's controls all logistics aspects of the Dior brand for a truly unique turnkey solution.

"Brink's transformed to meet Dior's requirements," said David Zerah, Global Services manager of Brink's France. "Our team demonstrated a commitment to quality, security, and enthusiasm from the get-go. We understood that managing Dior's logistics was a chance to showcase our abilities as a worldwide leader in secure logistics."

In London, Brink's joined forces with Goldsmiths' Company Assay Office London in 2008 to deliver a one-of-a-kind solution for jewelry customers—a premier hallmarking facility within the secure premises of Brink's Global Services at Heathrow Airport, United Kingdom. With this unique service, Brink's customers can receive the best hallmarking available without having to spend precious time on additional transportation.

Brink's highly secure premises house a luxury customer viewing room to facilitate quality control. The Assay Office London is complete with the latest hallmarking technology and equipment, including hand, press, and laser marking. "This is a state-of-the-art facility that offers a first-class through-packet solution from production to hallmarking to distribution with greater efficiency and lower security risks," said Eyal-Fibeesh. "International customers importing and exporting precious metals can reduce the number of steps in the supply chain, thus ultimately decreasing turnaround time. And we all know; time saved is money earned."

Also in London, Brink's has developed a unique solution to take on the entire cash operations of one of the world's largest financial services companies. The solution is a customer-specific cash center where Brink's consolidates all retail, wholesale, and ECI (Extended Custodial Inventory) currency activities into a single operation, making it possible for the customer to outsource all of its foreign and local currency management functions to Brink's. "Many of our customers outsource a portion of the cash operations to us," said Eyal-Fibeesh. "By thinking outside the box and working with the customer's unique specifications and requirements, we developed a unique solution that increases efficiency and security while shortening lead times and driving cost savings throughout the cash cycle."

In Colombia, South America, where population density and restricted use of vehicles in certain areas make secure transportation by truck difficult, if not impossible, the local Brink's team created Domesa de Colombia, a unique solution that transports noncash items, such as checks or ATM cards, by motorcycle.

"Mail service in Colombia is not as secure as it is in other countries," said Alberto Arciniegas, country manager for Brink's Colombia. "For example, here a bank might use Domesa to ensure customers get their credit cards or the checks they ordered."

Another service unique to Brink's Colombia, Procesos & Canje, provides back-office processing of both cash and noncash payments. Added Arciniegas, "With our traditional Cash in Transit service, Domesa, Procesos & Canje, and ePago International, we are able to provide a fully integrated payment solution, from point of sale or payment to reconciliation, that customers cannot get anywhere else."

A Bright Future

In Asia, Brink's Hong Kong expanded its services to the Macau region of China, a burgeoning center for the gambling industry. "You had all the famous brands of luxury goods arriving into Macau, and Brink's entered to serve the customers that we usually serve around the world, such as Tiffany, the Richman Group, and some other high-end jewelry and watches companies," said Amit Zukerman, president of Brink's Global Services. "The big casinos have opened up in Macau and made a big investment, and all the hotels that have served [the gambling industry] in the U.S. We saw it as an opportunity to go into the market."[42]

David Gronow, president of Brink's EMEA, believes Brink's next frontier is likely Africa. "We're looking at a number of new locations in Africa, particularly Egypt, Mauritania, and Algeria, and to the south, Tanzania and so forth, and also in the Ivory Coast (Côte d'Ivoire)," he said. "They're all works in progress at this point in time, but we're making very good progress in Madagascar, Mauritius, and Morocco. We're doing reasonably well out of the businesses that we established [in those countries] from 2005 through 2007."[43]

The fastest-growing regions for Brink's Global Services, according to Gronow, are "definitely the Middle East and the Gulf states and some aspects of the African continent, certainly across the top of the African continent. Egypt and Algeria are very much progressing at a rapid rate. Even countries

---

BRINK'S TODAY

THE BRINK'S OF TODAY LOOKS REMARKABLY different from the Brink's of the early days. Today, thousands of companies, including banks, governments, manufacturers, diamantaires, retailers, hospitals, and many others, trust Brink's with their most precious valuables.

Brink's Primary Products and Solutions (as of 2008):

- Air Courier
- Brink's Global Services
- Armored transportation
- ATM maintenance and repair
- Brink's CompuSafe® Service
- Brink's Document Destruction
- Cash Processing
- Check Imaging
- Coin Processing
- Diamonds and Jewelry Services (including Hallmarking)
- Diamonds & Jewelry Trade Show Management Services
- Precious Metals Inventory Management and Transportation Services
- Security Services
- Track & Trace
- Secure Data Solutions
- Web Information Tools
- Virtual Vault Services

such as Libya are progressing economically, but they're in various stages of maturity in terms of their development."[44]

Although a global recession affected customers in 2008, the immediate future remained bright at Brink's. According to David Garton, Brink's vice president for strategic development:

I don't know if I would go so far as to say that, in fact, we are recession-proof, but I think there is a certain amount of resilience. In an economic downturn like this, cash becomes more of a king than it is normally because debt is a problem. Credit card debt is a problem. People tend to deal more with cash, so there is more cash in circulation.

We are certainly seeing that. I think the financial crisis that the banks are experiencing on a global basis probably resulted in the distribution of more cash. I wouldn't go so far as to call it a run on the banks, but I think it was a measure to ensure that if there was a run, the banking system was positioned to handle that.

Garton said Brink's global geographic diversification has also helped Brink's weather changes in demand. "Certainly the Latin American economy and the Asian economy are much more cash-centric than Western Europe or North America would be," he said.

He foresees an increasing demand for Brink's services. "The financial crisis and shoring up the banks, the failure of banks and other financial institutions, would probably be neutral to positive for us. In the U.S., in particular, we tend to be the major supplier to the larger banks, and as smaller banks fail and get gobbled up by the larger banks, that's probably beneficial to us."[45]

Next 150 Years

Since the horse-and-buggy days, to the modern age, Brink's has always approached change

rationally and deliberately. This way of doing business is the legacy of Brink's founding father, Perry Brink, and it has been the driving force in the company's success over the past 150 years. From the company's national expansion in the 1920s, shepherded by former Brink's president John D. Allen, to the international expansion marshaled by current CEO Michael T. Dan, the company has transformed from its cartage days into an international market leader in an industry that it helped define and shape.

Today's Brink's is more than an armored transportation provider; it is a global provider of secure logistics services. With a footprint that extends across North America, Latin America, Asia, Europe, the Middle East, Africa, and Oceania, Brink's operations serve customers in 110 countries across six continents with an expansive array of business and security services.

"Although the next 150 years will test us in ways we can't even imagine, I am certain of a few things," said Michael Dan. "We will continue to grow the business, both technologically and geographically. We will continue to develop value in the Brink's brand, and we will continue to find creative and powerful solutions for our customers, whether their needs are modest or great."

Brink's strategic combination of conservatism and foresight has allowed the company to prosper through 150 years of economic growth, recession, depression, war, and countless global changes—a remarkable feat by any measure. Perhaps more remarkable, though, is the fact that through it all, Brink's has maintained a level of integrity that has, quite literally, set the standard. Throughout the world, the name "Brink's" is virtually synonymous with the concept of trust.

"Our customers, our partners, our employees, and our communities trust us to do what we say we will do, and to do it well," added Dan. "We consider it an honor, and an obligation, to uphold this trust in everything we do, every day of the year."

BRINK'S WORLDWIDE SERVICE COVERAGE

NORTH AMERICA
Aruba
Bahamas
Canada
Costa Rica
Curaçao
Dominican Republic
Guadeloupe
Guam
Jamaica
Martinique
Puerto Rico
Saipan
St. Croix
St. Kitts
St. Lucia
St. Maarten
St. Martin
St. Thomas
United States

LATIN AMERICA
Argentina
Bolivia

Brazil
Cayman Islands
Chile
Colombia
Ecuador
El Salvador
French Guiana
Guatemala
Honduras
Mexico
Panama
Peru
Uruguay
Venezuela

AFRICA
Angola
Botswana
Cameroon
Côte D'Ivoire
Democratic Republic of Congo
Egypt
Ghana
Gibraltar

Kazakhstan
Kenya
Kyrgyzstan
Lesotho
Madagascar
Mauritius
Mayotte
Morocco
Mozambique
Namibia
Réunion
Senegal
South Africa
Tajikstan
Tanzania
Uzbekistan
Zambia
Zimbabwe

MIDDLE EAST
Bahrain
Cyprus
Israel
Jordan

Kuwait
Lebanon
Qatar
Saudi Arabia
United Arab Emirates

EUROPE

Andorra
Armenia
Austria
Azerbaijan
Belgium
Bulgaria
Croatia
Czech Republic
Denmark
Estonia
Finland
France
Georgia
Germany
Greece
Hungary
Iceland
Ireland
Italy
Latvia
Liechtenstein
Lithuania
Luxembourg
Malta
Monaco
Netherlands
Norway
Poland
Portugal
Romania
Russia
Slovakia
Slovenia
Spain
Sweden
Switzerland
Turkey
Ukraine

ASIA PACIFIC

Australia
Bangladesh
Brunei
Cambodia
China
East Timor
Fiji
French Polynesia–Tahiti
Hong Kong
India
Indonesia
Japan
Laos
Macau
Malaysia
Mongolia
Nepal
New Caledonia
New Zealand
Pakistan
Papua New Guinea
Philippines
Samoa
Singapore
South Korea
Sri Lanka
Taiwan
Thailand
Vietnam

BRINK'S FALLEN HEROES

BRINK'S EMPLOYEES WHO GAVE THEIR LIVES IN THE LINE OF DUTY

YEAR	EMPLOYEE	COUNTRY	YEAR	EMPLOYEE	COUNTRY
1917	Barton C. Allen	United States	1984	Robert Persowich	Canada
	Louis C. Osenberg	United States	1985	Alain Dessy	France
1924	Franklin Good	United States		Marcel Limoges	France
1949	Joseph Den	United States		Alain Merle	France
	Joseph Koziel	United States		Gilbert Secki	France
1969	Real Champagne	Canada	1986	Edson Machado Faleiro	Brazil
	John Glendinning	United States		Jose Edson de Souza	Brazil
	Joseph Martin	United States		Jean Pierre Variera	France
1970	Bertolino Ferreira	Brazil	1987	Anacleto Méndez	Colombia
	George J. Schnender	United States		Elias Gomes Pereira	Brazil
1971	Gerald Creaney, Jr.	United States	1988	Luis A. Yánquez De la Cerda	Chile
	Stanley P. Kaniuk	United States		Marco Antonio Garcia	Brazil
	Dov Livne	Israel		Rodrigo Campos Parra	Chile
	Gerald T. O'Connor	United States		Edison Enedino da Silva	Brazil
1972	Harold Baddeley	United States		Aldo Roman Toro	Chile
1973	Claude Vienneau	Canada		Gonzalo Santelices	
1974	Juul Busschots	Netherlands		Von der Knesebeck	Chile
	Adolph Potvin	Canada	1989	Joseph Arriola	United States
1975	Eugene Forton	United States	1990	Jolle Jansma	Netherlands
	Don Jones	United States	1991	Rick Bridgman	Canada
1977	Carl Simonsen	United States		Richard Germany	United States
1978	Pablo Sánchez	Venezuela		Gerardo Gonzáles Magni	Peru
1979	Raymond Dubois	France		Benjamin Roa	Venezuela
	Jorge Luis Junior	Brazil	1992	Bernardo Loza Aguayo	Chile
	Maurice Prudhomme	Canada		Antonio Toledo Leal	Venezuela
	Claude Thiroloix	France		Luis Espinoza Martínez	Venezuela
1980	Detlev Driebel	Germany		Oliver Ortiz	Colombia
	Paul Martinez	United States	1993	Everett (Eddie) Hall	United States
	Larry Roberts	Canada		Luis Jose Aaron Maestre	Colombia
	William Sieg	United States	1994	Roberto Custodio de Souza	Brazil
	Wolfgang Simmler	Germany		Celso de Souza Lima	Brazil
	Luis Toledo	Venezuela		Manuel Garcia Araya	Chile
	Raymond Vince	Canada		Abel Gonzales	United States
1981	William Moroney	United States		Charles Norris	United States
	Peter Paige	United States		Dennie Plese	United States
1982	Nelson Araujo	Brazil		Freddy Mendoza Ramos	Colombia
	Newton Mello Kallut Filho	Brazil		Jeffrey Spencer	United States
	Joe Warner	United States	1995	Herman Dwight Cook	United States
1983	Yvon Charland	Canada		Jimmie Hill	United States
	Helio Malentachi	Brazil		Oscar Mauricio Morales Monsalve	Colombia
	Luis Germano Sabino	Brazil		Marco Tulio Marentes	Colombia

YEAR	EMPLOYEE	COUNTRY
1995	Larry Espinosa	United States
	Jairo Guacapino	Colombia
	John Hamilton	United States
	Fernando Herrera	United States
	Didier Mazingue	France
	Mario Jose Souza da Costa	Brazil
1996	Muhammad Afzal	Pakistan
	Robert Belcher	United States
	Daney Castillo	Colombia
	Gustavo Neil Flores Ochoa	Peru
	Arif Hussain	Pakistan
	Ahmed Khan	Pakistan
	Mark Smith	United States
1997	Vanderval Ferreira de Lucena	Brazil
	Ivan Lecomte	Luxembourg
	Louis Vermeire	Belgium
1998	Alberto de Jesús Acousta Morales	Colombia
	Maqsood Ahmed	Pakistan
	Jean-Jacques Amadei	France
	Muhammad Azam	Pakistan
	Acacio Januario de Carvalho	Brazil
	Benny De Meester	Belgium
	Arturo Yanquez de la Cerda	Chile
	Gulzar Hussain	Pakistan
	Koenraad Meirens	Belgium
	Román Pacacio Mosquera	Colombia
	Hussain Mubashir	Pakistan
	Louis Voerman	France
	William Strelow	United States
	Jean-Pierre Gorvel	France
1999	Nelson Darío Cabrera Cardenas	Colombia
	Elzear Jaramillo	United States
	Jean-Luc Lutard	France
	Roberto Rodríguez	Venezuela
	Fabiano Jose da Silva Ramos	Brazil
	Miriam Zapata Ramírez	Chile
2000	Manuel José Delgado	Colombia
	Sergio Leite Dos Santos	Brazil
	Michel Guiot	Luxembourg
	Zulfigar Hussain	Pakistan
	Tanosh Khan	Pakistan
	Marco Antonio Kutitiake	Brazil
	Alexandre Henrique Moreiro	Brazil
	Fernando Obregon Castro	Chile
	Jhon Hoover Perea	Colombia
	Luis Alberto Rojas	Colombia
	Samuel Saenz	United States
	Ronald D. Trott	United States
2001	Antonio Vicente Ayala Banquero	Colombia
	Reinaldo Camargo	Venezuela
	Ignacio Delgado	United States
	Ricardo Gomez	United States
	Hernan Dario Gonzalez	Colombia
	Jean-Luc Hulot	France

YEAR	EMPLOYEE	COUNTRY
2001	Eric J. Rigney	United States
	José Gregorio Rodríguez	Venezuela
	Juan Carlos Salazar	Colombia
	Wallace Terrell	United States
	Francis Joseph Trombino	United States
2002	José Guerrero Cid	Chile
	Fernandes da Silva Lima	Brazil
	Darren James Daine	Canada
	Dena Daniels	United States
	Guillermo Orjuela Espinosa	Colombia
	Mark Grossman	United States
	Argenis Francisco Lugo	Venezuela
	Lionel Marsalle	France
	Adelino Moura dos Santos	Brazil
	Silvestre Vasquez	Brazil
2003	Shannon Angerome	United States
	Eslli De Castro	Brazil
	Antonio Demecio Zacarias	Venezuela
	José Carlos dos Santos	Brazil
	Edgardo Santos	Panama
	Rafael Yacson Maraguacare	Venezuela
2004	Mordechay Cohen	Israel
	Dimas Sudario Ferreira	Brazil
	Wilmer Gonzalez	Venezuela
	Carlos Alberto Lemus Rodriguez	Colombia
	Corey Bo Medlock	United States
	Milton Moran	United States
	Silei Basposa Santana	Brazil
2005	Jack Ronnie Peterson	Brazil
	Jose Roberto Picinato	Brazil
	Carlos Roberto Rossi	Brazil
2006	Joao Batista Barbosa	Brazil
	Raúl Flores	Panama
	Rofer Gutierrez	Venezuela
	Michale Manigel	Germany
	Ricaurte Ortega	Panama
	Paulo Rodrigues de Oliveira	Brazil
	Antonio J. Quintero	United States
	Max Sanchez	Panama
2007	Clement Acina	France
	Gazdig Laszlo	Hungary
	Antonio Orlando Murua	Argentina
2008	Rueben Alonzo Quinto	Venezuela
	Delicia Averez	Bolivia
	Pablo Contreras	Columbia
	Miguel Quintero	Columbia
	Douglas Rosas	Venezuela
	Juan Salado	United States
	Efrain Santaella	Venezuela
2009	Jean Carlos Vivas Rodriquez	Venezuela

NOTES TO SOURCES

Chapter One

1. Theodore J. Karamanski, *Rally 'Round the Flag: Chicago and the Civil War*, (Lanham, Maryland: Rowman & Littlefield Publishers, Inc., 2006), xi.
2. James L. Dunbar and Robert Grant Kingwell, *Bulletproof: A History of Armored Cars and the Colorful Characters Who Ran Them, Rode Them, and Sometimes Robbed Them*, (Hunt Valley, Maryland: Mid Atlantic Books & Journals, 2003), 16–17.
3. R. A. Seng and J. V. Gilmour, *Brink's—The Money Movers: The Story of a Century of Service*, (Chicago: Brink's Inc., 1959), 17; *Brink's Story Book 2004: Histoire de Brink's*, (France: Brink's France, 2003).
4. Edward L. Gavin, *Washington Perry Brink: Founder of Brink's Inc.*, (Self-published family genealogy).
5. *Brink's—The Money Movers*, 18.
6. Harold M. Mayer and Richard C. Wade, *Chicago: Growth of a Metropolis*, (Chicago and London: The University of Chicago Press, 1969), 98.
7. *Chicago: Growth of a Metropolis*, 94, 96.
8. Ibid., 96, 98.
9. *Brink's—The Money Movers*, 19.
10. Ibid., 19.
11. *Rally 'Round the Flag*, 6–7.
12. *Brink's—The Money Movers*, 21.
13. Ibid., 6.
14. *Rally 'Round the Flag*, 17.
15. Ibid., 28–30.
16. Classified ad, *Chicago Tribune*, 30 April 1868, 4.
17. Classified ad, *Chicago Tribune*, 11 May 1868, 1; Classified ad, *Chicago Tribune*, 8 March 1870, 1.
18. Classified ad, *Chicago Tribune*, 22 May 1870, 1.
19. Forrest Crissey, *Moving Money*, (Chicago: Brink's Express Company, Inc., 1929), 16; Classified ad, *Chicago Tribune*, 8 March 1870, 4.
20. Ibid., 16.
21. Ibid.
22. Ibid., 16–17.
23. Ibid.
24. Ibid., 34–35.
25. "Mad Dog in a House: Rabid Creature Rushes into the Modjeski Residence," *Chicago Tribune*, 28 July 1894, 1.
26. Classified ad, *Chicago Tribune*, 14 September 1871, 4.
27. Classified ad, *Chicago Tribune*, 12 July 1871, 1.
28. *Chicago: Growth of a Metropolis*, 106.
29. Ibid.
30. *Brink's—The Money Movers*, 10.
31. *Chicago: Growth of a Metropolis*, 117.
32. Classified ad, *Chicago Tribune*, 17 October 1871, 1.

Chapter One Sidebar: An Early Focus on Safety

1. Forrest Crissey, *Moving Money*, (Chicago: Brink's Express Company, Inc., 1929), 16; Classified ad, *Chicago Tribune*, 8 March 1870, 18–19.
2. Ibid.
3. Ibid., 20.
4. R. A. Seng and J. V. Gilmour, *Brink's—The Money Movers: The Story of a Century of Service*, (Chicago: Brink's Inc., 1959), 23–24.

Chapter One Sidebar: Perry's Mysterious Partners

1. Edward L. Gavin, *Washington Perry Brink: Founder of Brink's Inc.*, (Self-published family genealogy); Classified ad, *Chicago Tribune*, 22 May 1870, 1.
2. Classified ad, *Chicago Tribune*, 12 July 1871, 1; Classified ad, *Chicago Tribune*, 18 September 1872, 5.
3. Classified ad, *Chicago Tribune*, 5 January 1873, 4.
4. "The City," *Chicago Tribune*, 12 May 1880, 8.

Chapter Two

1. Harold M. Mayer and Richard C. Wade, *Chicago: Growth of a Metropolis*, (Chicago and London: The University of Chicago Press, 1969), 117.
2. Ibid., 120, 122.
3. Bessie Louise Pierce, *As Others See Chicago: Impressions of Visitors, 1673–1933*, (Chicago: The University of Chicago Press, 2004), 208.
4. Classified ad, *Chicago Tribune*, 12 June 1872, 6.
5. Classified ad, *Chicago Tribune*, 4 August 1872, 1.
6. *Frederick Law Olmsted, Founder of Landscape Architecture*, http://www.fredericklawolmsted.com/.
7. Classified ad, *Chicago Tribune*, 7 April 1872, 4.
8. Ibid.
9. Classified ad, *Chicago Tribune*, 27 November 1872, 5.
10. Classified ad, *Chicago Tribune*, 28 August 1872, 5.
11. Edward L. Gavin, *Washington Perry Brink: Founder of Brink's Inc.*, (Self-published family genealogy).
12. Obituary, *Chicago Tribune*, 24 July 1874.
13. R. A. Seng and J. V. Gilmour, *Brink's—The Money Movers: The Story*

of a Century of Service, (Chicago: Brink's Inc., 1959), 17.

14. "Death of George W. French," *Chicago Tribune*, 5 January 1891, 3.

15. James R. Grossman, Ann Durkin Keating, and Janice L. Reiff, editors, *The Encyclopedia of Chicago* (Chicago: The Newberry Library, 2004), 828, 831.

16. Forrest Crissey, *Moving Money*, (Chicago: Brink's Express Company, Inc., 1929), 9.

17. *Brink's—The Money Movers: The Story of a Century of Service*, 25–26.

18. *Moving Money*, 32.

19. *Brink's—The Money Movers*, 24.

20. *Moving Money*, 32.

21. *Brink's—The Money Movers*, 24.

22. "Byron Schermerhorn: The First President, Businessman, Poet, Civil War Intelligence Agent," *Brink's Link*, Fall 2001, 8–9.

23. The Lakeside Chicago, Illinois, General & Business Directories for 1881 and 1882, (Chicago: The Chicago City Directory Company, 1881 and 1882).

24. "Byron Schermerhorn: The First President, Businessman, Poet, Civil War Intelligence Agent," 8–9.

25. Ibid.

26. Barbara Ryan, editor, "Genealogical Information from the Hinsdale Doings," 15 January 1898, and 9 April 1898.

27. *Brink's—The Money Movers*, 26.

28. *Brink's—The Money Movers*, 27.

29. The Lakeside Chicago, Illinois, General & Business Directory for 1881.

30. *Encyclopedia of Chicago*, 679.

31. Arthur B. Tebbets and Frank M. Simmons, editors, *History of Ravenswood*, (Chicago: Mirror Publishing Company, 1898).

32. *The Chicago Blue Book of Selected Names of Chicago and Suburban Towns*, (Chicago: The Chicago Directory Company, 1909).

33. *Chicago Tribune*, 29 March 1894, 8.

34. Ibid.

35. Classified ad, *Chicago Tribune*, 12 March 1882, 8.

36. *Encyclopedia of Chicago*, 375.

37. "To Charge 50 Cents for Carting Trunks," *Chicago Tribune*, 25 March 1892, 3.

38. *Encyclopedia of Chicago*, B30.

39. Bruce H. Moshe, "The Stamps of the Brink's Chicago City Express Company," *Scott Stamp Monthly*, August 1998, Vol. 16, No. 8, 68–71, 86.

40. *Brink's—The Money Movers*, 28.

41. *Moving Money*, 18.

42. *Brink's—The Money Movers*, 29.

43. *Moving Money*, 17–18.

44. Ibid., 33.

45. *Encyclopedia of Chicago*, 898–902.

46. *Moving Money*, 33.

47. *Encyclopedia of Chicago*, B30.

48. Classified ad, *Chicago Tribune*, 15 April 1894, 24.

**Chapter Two Sidebar:
Stamped, Sealed, and Delivered**

1. Bruce H. Moshen, "The Stamps of the Brink's Chicago City Express Company," *Scott Stamp Monthly*, August 1998, Vol. 16, No. 8, 68–71, 86.

2. Ibid.

3. Ibid.

**Chapter Two Sidebar:
Horse Tales**

1. Forrest Crissey, *Moving Money*, (Chicago: Brink's Express Company, Inc., 1929), 22–23.

2. *Moving Money*, 23.

3. Forrest Crissey, *The Romance of Moving Money*, (Chicago: The Library of Institutional Biography, 1934), 22.

4. Ibid., 21–22.

5. "A Runaway Horse's Mischief," *Chicago Tribune*, 31 August 1888, 1.

6. "Items," *Chicago Tribune*, 22 November 1888, 9.

7. *Moving Money*, 23.

Chapter Three

1. Forrest Crissey, *The Romance of Moving Money*, (Chicago: The Library of Institutional Biography, 1934), 41.

2. R. A. Seng and J. V. Gilmour, *Brink's—The Money Movers: The Story of a Century of Service*, (Chicago: Brink's Inc., 1959), 38.

3. Jeffrey S. Adler, *First in Violence, Deepest in Dirt: Homicide in Chicago 1875–1920*, (Cambridge: Harvard University Press, 2006), 244.

4. Ibid., 250.

5. *Brink's Story Book 2004: Histoire de Brink's*, (France: Brink's France, 2003).

6. James R. Grossman, Ann Durkin Keating, and Janice L. Reiff, editors, *The Encyclopedia of Chicago*, (Chicago: The Newberry Library, 2004).

7. *Brink's—The Money Movers*, 42.

8. Ibid., 31–32.

9. Forrest Crissey, *Moving Money*, (Chicago: Brink's Express Company, Inc., 1929), 16; Classified ad, *Chicago Tribune*, 8 March 1870, 33.

10. *Brink's—The Money Movers*, 40.

11. "Brink's Acquires 1904 Air-Cooled Delivery Wagon—Our First Truck,"

Brink's Link, Vol. 22, No. 28, Summer 1997, 1.

12. *Brink's—The Money Movers*, 44.

13. Ibid., 43.

14. *First in Violence, Deepest in Dirt*, 246.

15. Ibid., 245.

16. Ibid., 241.

17. Ibid., 253.

18. Ibid., 248.

19. "Brink Sells Residence," *Chicago Tribune*, 29 April 1910, 13.

20. *Brink's—The Money Movers*, 43.

21 "Brink's Family Comes into Focus," *Brink's Link*, Vol. X, No. 31, Spring 1995, 2.

22. Ibid.

23. Ibid., 1.

24. Ibid., 4.

25. *Brink's—The Money Movers*, 40-41.

26. James L. Dunbar and Robert Grant Kingwell, *Bulletproof: A History of Armored Cars and the Colorful Characters Who Ran Them, Rode Them, and Sometimes Robbed Them*, (Hunt Valley, Maryland: Mid Atlantic Books & Journals, 2003), 42.

27. *Brink's—The Money Movers*, 43.

28. *The Romance of Moving Money*, 38.

29. "Brink's, Incorporated, Celebrating Its Centennial Year, 1859–1959," press release, 27 April 1959, 9.

30. *Moving Money*, 24.

31. "Gang Held in Fatal Holdup Battles Cops," *Chicago Tribune*, 29 August 1917, 1.

32. *The Romance of Moving Money*, 44–45.

33. "Get Slayer in Two Hour Battle," *Chicago Tribune*, 31 August 1917, 1.

34. "Gang Held in Fatal Holdup Battles Cops."

35. "Get Slayer in Two Hour Battle."

36. Ibid.

37. Ibid.

38. "Three Bandits Confess All," *Chicago Tribune*, 1 September 1917, 1.

39. "Capture Fifth of Bandits; Only One Now At Large," *Chicago Tribune*, 2 September 1917, 7.

40. *The Romance of Moving Money*, 46.

41. "Lindrum and Wheed Die on Jail Scaffold," *Chicago Tribune*, 16 February 1918, 8.

42. *Moving Money*, 24.

43. *Bulletproof*, 24.

44. *The Romance of Moving Money*, 39–40; *First in Violence, Deepest in Dirt*, 246.

45. *Encyclopedia of Chicago*, 133.

46. *The Romance of Moving Money*, 41.

**Chapter Three Sidebar:
Frank Allen**

1. R. A. Seng and J. V. Gilmour, *Brink's—The Money Movers: The Story of a*

Century of Service, (Chicago: Brink's Inc., 1959), 40–41.
2. Sam B. Lyons, "Half Century with Brink's, Inc.," *Finance*, Vol. 67, No. 2, 15 August 1954.
3. *Brink's—The Money Movers*, 41.
4. "Death Notices," *Chicago Tribune*, 30 August 1917, 15.
5. *Brink's—The Money Movers*, 47–48.

Chapter Three Sidebar:
The Evolution of Brink's Motorized Fleet

1. Larry Gormally, "Brink's Company Truck Restoration," *Springfield Journal*, 17 July 1997, Vol. 23, No. 1, 1.
2. John Keebler II, "Knox: The Perfect Car," *Automobile Quarterly*, Vol. 20, No. 2.
3. "Brink's Acquires 1904 Air-Cooled Delivery Wagon—Our First Truck," *Brink's Link*, Vol. 22, No. 28, Summer 1997, 4.
4. Ibid., 5–6.
5. Ibid., 4–5.
6. Ibid., 6.
7. Ibid., 4–5.
8. Ibid., 6.
9. James L. Dunbar and Robert Grant Kingwell, *Bulletproof: A History of Armored Cars and the Colorful Characters Who Ran Them, Rode Them, and Sometimes Robbed Them*, (Hunt Valley, Maryland: Mid Atlantic Books & Journals, 2003), 35.
10. R. A. Seng and J. V. Gilmour, *Brink's—The Money Movers: The Story of a Century of Service*, (Chicago: Brink's Inc., 1959), 66.
11. *Brink's Story Book 2004: Histoire de Brink's*, (France: Brink's France, 2003).

Chapter Three Sidebar:
Wanted

1. Forrest Crissey, *Moving Money*, (Chicago: Brink's Express Company, Inc., 1929), 16; Classified ad, *Chicago Tribune*, 8 March 1870, 24.
2. R. A. Seng and J. V. Gilmour, *Brink's—The Money Movers: The Story of a Century of Service*, (Chicago: Brink's Inc., 1959), 79.
3. Sam B. Lyons, "Half Century with Brink's, Inc.," *Finance*, Vol. 67, No. 2, 15 August 1954.

Chapter Four

1. Gilbert K. Chesterton, "The Gunman and the Racketeer," *As Others See Chicago: Impressions of Visitors, 1673–1933*, Bessie Louise Pierce, editor, (Chicago: University of Chicago Press, 2004), 500.

2. "The Birth of the BTC," *Brink's Link*, Spring 1996, Vol. XI, No. 34; R. A. Seng and J. V. Gilmour, *Brink's—The Money Movers: The Story of a Century of Service*, (Chicago: Brink's Inc., 1959), 46.
3. James L. Dunbar and Robert Grant Kingwell, *Bulletproof: A History of Armored Cars and the Colorful Characters Who Ran Them, Rode Them, and Sometimes Robbed Them*, (Hunt Valley, Maryland: Mid Atlantic Books & Journals, 2003), 51.
4. "The Birth of the BTC," 4.
5. *Brink's—The Money Movers*, 50.
6. Brink's company archives.
7. Sam B. Lyons, "Half Century with Brink's, Inc.," *Finance*, Vol. 67, No. 2, 15 August 1954.
8. Brink's company archives.
9. *Brink's—The Money Movers*, 46.
10. *Bulletproof*, 79.
11. Ibid., 50.
12. Otto Plank, "Man, How Time Flies," *Brink's Messenger*, Summer 1954.
13. Brink's company archives.
14. *Brink's—The Money Movers*, 50–51.
15. Brink's company archives.
16. Ibid.
17. *Brink's—The Money Movers*, 49.
18. Ibid., 54.
19. Ibid., 49.
20. Brink's Museum, Chicago.
21. *Brink's—The Money Movers*, 49.
22. Brink's archives, Frank D. Allen Collection.
23. Brink's company archives.
24. Ibid.
25. *Brink's—The Money Movers*, 53.
26. *Bulletproof*, 68.
27. Forrest Crissey, *Moving Money*, (Chicago: Brink's Express Company, Inc., 1929).
28. *Brink's Story Book 2004: Histoire de Brink's*, (France: Brink's France, 2003).
29. Brink's company archives.
30. International Harvester ad, *The Literary Digest*, reproduced in *Brink's Link*, Summer 2000, Vol. XV, No. 50, 15.
31. *Brink's—The Money Movers*, 75–76.
32. Advertisement, *Chicago Tribune*, 26 July 1920, 18.
33. Brink's company archives.
34. *Brink's Story Book 2004*.
35. Brink's company archives.
36. *Bulletproof*, 105.
37. *Moving Money*, 39.
38. Two-Key Safe display, Brink's Museum.
39. "Hunt Beer Gang as Bandits," *Chicago Tribune*, 11 September 1926, 1.
40. Herbert Asbury, *The Gangs of Chicago: An Informal History of the Chicago Underworld*, (New York: Thunder's Mouth Press, 2002), 325.

41. "Hunt Beer Gang as Bandits," 1.
42. Ibid.
43. Forrest Crissey, *The Romance of Moving Money*, (Chicago: The Library of Institutional Biography, 1934), 98.
44. Uniform display, Brink's Museum, Chicago.
45. Ibid.
46. *Moving Money*, 41–42.
47. Ibid., 42–43.
48. Brink's company archives.

Chapter Four Sidebar:
John D. Allen

1. Sam B. Lyons, "Half Century with Brink's, Inc.," *Finance*, Vol. 67, No. 2, 15 August 1954.
2. Ibid.
3. "Brink's Express President Buys Country Estate," *Chicago Tribune*, 13 February 1927, B2.
4. "Ministers to Meet Again Tomorrow," *Chicago Tribune*, 9 September 1928, H10.
5. "Episcopal Laymen Name John D. Allen President of Club," *Chicago Tribune*, 16 June 1929, J5.
6. *Brink's Messenger*, Summer 1952, Vol. 1, No. 1, 2.

Chapter Four Sidebar:
The Coverdale Robbery

1. H. Edward Reeves, "The Great Coverdale Robbery," *Brink's Messenger*, Summer 1954, 9.
2. Ibid.
3. "Bandits Dynamite Armored Pay Car and Take $104,250," *New York Times*, 12 March 1927.
4. "The Great Coverdale Robbery," 9.
5. Rich Sebah, "Gangster History in Bethel Park," *Pittsburgh Magazine*, March 2007.
6. Forrest Crissey, *The Romance of Moving Money*, (Chicago: The Library of Institutional Biography, 1934), 98.

Chapter Five

1. "$50 Million Cash a Day Handled by Express Co.," *Chicago Tribune*, 11 March 1933, 6.
2. James R. Grossman, Ann Durkin Keating, and Janice L. Reiff, editors, *The Encyclopedia of Chicago*, (Chicago: The Newberry Library, 2004), 360.
3. Roger Biles, *Big City Boss in Depression and War: Mayor Edward J. Kelly of Chicago*, (Dekalb, Illinois: Northern Illinois University Press, 1984), 21.
4. Ibid., 22.
5. *Encyclopedia of Chicago*, 360.
6. Charles J. Masters, *Governor Henry Horner, Chicago Politics, and the Great*

Depression, (Carbondale, Illinois: Southern Illinois University Press, 2007).

7. Randall E. Parker, *The Economics of the Great Depression: A Twenty-First Century Look Back at the Economics of the Interwar Era*, (Northampton, Massachusetts: Edward Elgar, 2007), 6, 8–9; Anthony J. Badger, *The New Deal: The Depression Years, 1933–1940*, (Chicago: Ivan R. Dee, 2002), 69.

8. *The Economics of the Great Depression*, 179.

9. *The New Deal*, 69.

10. Forrest Crissey, *The Romance of Moving Money*, (Chicago: The Library of Institutional Biography, 1934), 30.

11. R. A. Seng and J. V. Gilmour, *Brink's—The Money Movers: The Story of a Century of Service*, (Chicago: Brink's Inc., 1959), 56.

12. Susan Estabrook Kennedy, *The Banking Crisis of 1933*, (Lexington, Kentucky: University Press of Kentucky, 1973), 77.

13. *The Romance of Moving Money*, 31.

14. Ibid.

15. Ibid., 30.

16. "Accounts Handled Here for Michigan," *New York Times*, 16 February 1933.

17. *The Banking Crisis of 1933*, 96.

18. Elmus Wicker, *The Banking Panics of the Great Depression*, (New York: Cambridge University Press, 1996), 121.

19. *Brink's—The Money Movers*, 57.

20. Ibid., 57–58.

21. "$50 Million Cash a Day Handled by Express Co.," 6

22. *Brink's—The Money Movers*, 58.

23. Ibid., 59.

24. Ibid., 92.

25. Brink's company archives.

26. Ibid.

27. Ibid.

28. Ibid.

29. Ibid.

30. *Brink's—The Money Movers*, 89–90.

31. Ibid., 89.

32. Brink's company archives.

33. "Investors Guide," *Chicago Tribune*, 1 November 1938, 28.

34. *Brink's—The Money Movers*, 111–112.

35. Al Chase, "Cash Fortress Will Be Built by Brink Company," *Chicago Tribune*, 3 October 1937, B9.

36. Brink's 1939 Annual Report.

37. Brink's company archives.

38. *The Romance of Moving Money*, 104.

39. Brink's company archives.

40. Otto Plank, "Man, How Time Flies," *Brink's Messenger*, Summer 1954.

41. Brink's 1943 Annual Report.

42. Brink's 1944 Annual Report.

43. James L. Dunbar and Robert Grant Kingwell, *Bulletproof: A History of Armored Cars and the Colorful Characters Who Ran Them, Rode Them, and Sometimes Robbed Them*, (Hunt Valley, Maryland: Mid Atlantic Books & Journals, 2003), 160.

44. Brink's 1941 Annual Report.

45. "Banking Weekly to Get New Name," *New York Times*, 6 June 1941.

46. *Encyclopedia of Chicago*.

47. "Horses and Courses," *Time Magazine*, 3 August 1936.

48. "Board Accepts $1,600,000 for Arlington," *Chicago Tribune*, 16 April 1940, 19.

49. "Chicagoans Buying Estate Properties in Woodstock in McHenry County," *Chicago Tribune*, 25 April 1937, C18.

50. "City Residents Buy Thousands of Acres for Farming in the Libertyville Area," *Chicago Tribune*, 30 June 1937, C14.

51. "Kelly to Name J. D. Allen to School Board," *Chicago Tribune*, 14 June 1939, 1.

52. "John D. Allen Resigns from School Board," *Chicago Tribune*, 15 July 1939, 10.

53. Brink's company archives.

54. Brink's 1946 Annual Report.

55. *Brink's—The Money Movers*, 92.

56. *Brink's Story Book 2004: Histoire de Brink's*, (France: Brink's France, 2003).

Chapter Five Sidebar:
Century of Progress World's Fair

1. "New Scenes Rise When Midnight Dims Fair Lights," *Chicago Tribune*, 25 June 1933, 3.

2. James R. Grossman, Ann Durkin Keating, and Janice L. Reiff, editors, *The Encyclopedia of Chicago*, (Chicago: The Newberry Library, 2004), 124–125.

3. Ibid., 125.

Chapter Five Sidebar:
Safecrackers

1. "Robbers Force Victims to Put Safe on Truck," *Chicago Tribune*, 11 August 1930, 1.

2. "Iron Workers Union's Safe Resists Efforts of Yeggs," *Chicago Tribune*, 28 June 1938, 10.

Chapter Five Sidebar:
War Rationing

1. "How to Get a Tire," *Time*, 12 January 1942.

2. "220 West Siders Get Permits for 830 New Tires, 633 Tubes," *Chicago Tribune*, 11 October 1942, W4.

3. James L. Dunbar and Robert Grant Kingwell, *Bulletproof: A History of Armored Cars and the Colorful Characters Who Ran Them, Rode Them, and Sometimes Robbed Them*, (Hunt Valley, Maryland: Mid Atlantic Books & Journals, 2003), 160.

4. "OPA Moves Gas, Tire Coupons to New Offices," *Chicago Tribune*, 16 August 1944, 3.

5. *Bulletproof*, 235.

6. Brink's 1941 Annual Report.

Chapter Five Sidebar:
The *Spitfire*

1. James L. Dunbar and Robert Grant Kingwell, *Bulletproof: A History of Armored Cars and the Colorful Characters Who Ran Them, Rode Them, and Sometimes Robbed Them*, (Hunt Valley, Maryland: Mid Atlantic Books & Journals, 2003), 157–158, 160.

2. Ibid., 172.

Chapter Six

1. Sid Feder and Joseph F. Dinneen, *The Great Brink's Holdup*, (Garden City, New York: Doubleday & Company, 1961).

2. "Man Who Figured Job Sought Here," *Boston Daily Globe*, 18 January 1950.

3. "Bulletins," *Boston Daily Globe*, 18 January 1950.

4. "Man Who Figured Job Sought Here."

5. "Trace Holdup Cars," *Boston Daily Globe*, 18 January 1950, 1.

6. "Brink's Heist Informer Dies," *New York Times*, 28 March 1976.

7. "'Couldn't Believe My Eyes,' Says Messenger of Gunmen's Invasion," *Boston Daily Globe*, 18 January 1950, 14.

8. Ibid.

9. "Brink's Heist Informer Dies."

10. "Man Who Figured Job Sought Here."

11. "Trace Holdup Cars."

12. David Kapella, interview by Jeffrey L. Rodengen, digital recording, 22 April 2008, Write Stuff Enterprises, Inc.

13. "Brink's Heist Informer Dies."

14. Ibid.

15. "Famous Cases: The Brink's Robbery," Federal Bureau of Investigation, http://www.fbi.gov/libref/historic/famcases/brinks/brinks.htm/.

16. Sam B. Lyons, "Half Century with Brink's, Inc.," *Finance*, Vol. 67, No. 2, 15 August 1954.

17. "Massachusetts Passes Brink's Bill," *Brink's Messenger*, Autumn 1955.

18. "Brink's Heist Informer Dies."
19. James L. Dunbar and Robert Grant Kingwell, *Bulletproof: A History of Armored Cars and the Colorful Characters Who Ran Them, Rode Them, and Sometimes Robbed Them*, (Hunt Valley, Maryland: Mid Atlantic Books & Journals, 2003), 203.
20. "Brink's Heist Informer Dies."
21. "J. D. Says," *Brink's Messenger*, Winter 1956.
22. "Brink's Holdup Solved," *Brink's Messenger*, Winter 1956.
23. Brink's 1955 Annual Report.
24. Ibid.
25. Noel Behn, *Big Stick-Up At Brink's!*, (New York: G. P. Putnam's Sons, 1977), 371, 376.
26. "Trial of Boston Robbery Suspects Delayed," *Brink's Messenger*, Spring 1956.
27. "Trial of Boston Robbery Suspects Under Way," *Brink's Messenger*, Summer 1956.
28. Ibid.
29. "Brink's Heist Informer Dies."
30. R. A. Seng and J. V. Gilmour, *Brink's—The Money Movers: The Story of a Century of Service*, (Chicago: Brink's Inc., 1959), 104–105.
31. Ibid., 105–107.
32. "The End of the Road," *Brink's Messenger*, Winter 1956–57.
33. Ibid.
34. *How to Meet the Press*, Brink's Inc. public relations handbook, 1952.
35. Ibid.
36. "Brink's Heist Informer Dies."
37. "Last Brink's Robber Leaves State Prison," *Newport News*, 4 June 1970.
38. Brink's 1950 Annual Report.
39. Ibid.
40. Brink's 1951 Annual Report.
41. Brink's company archives.
42. Brink's 1952 Annual Report.
43. Brink's 1953 Annual Report.
44. Brink's 1952 Annual Report.
45. Ibid.
46. Ibid.
47. "J. D. Says," *Brink's Messenger*, Summer 1952.
48. Brink's 1953 Annual Report.
49. Brink's 1952 Annual Report.
50. "J. D. Says," *Brink's Messenger*, Autumn 1955.
51. "The President Looks at Our 1955 Operations," *Brink's Messenger*, Spring 1956.
52. "J. D. Says," *Brink's Messenger*, Autumn 1955.
53. Brink's 1955 Annual Report.
54. Brink's 1956 Annual Report.
55. Brink's 1957 Annual Report.
56. "New Coin Hauling Service Starts," *Brink's Messenger*, Spring 1955.

57. *Bulletproof*, 199.
58. *Brink's—The Money Movers*, 93.
59. "President Murphy Reports on 1956 and Looks Ahead," *Brink's Messenger*, Spring 1957.
60. Brink's 1951 Annual Report.
61. "Clink, Clink, Clink Go the Parking Meters," *Brink's Messenger*, Winter 1954–55.
62. *Brink's—The Money Movers*, 94.
63. "New Trends in Armored Car Service," *Brink's Messenger*, Autumn 1955.
64. *Brink's—The Money Movers*, 113.
65. Joseph P. Routh, *The Pittston Company: A Bright Future in Energy*, (New York: The Newcomen Society in North America, 1956), 7–8.
66. Ibid.
67. Ibid.
68. Ibid.
69. The Pittston Company 1956 Annual Report.
70. Ibid.
71. George Holl, interview by Jeffrey L. Rodengen, digital recording, 24 July 2008, Write Stuff Enterprises, Inc.

**Chapter Six Sidebar:
False Leads**

1. "Dig at Racetrack for Holdup Loot," *Boston Daily Record*, 24 January 1950.
2. "Masks on Sale in Boston Store," *Boston Post*, 19 January 1950.
3. "Question Man in Winthrop," *Boston Post*, 19 January 1950.
4. "Brink's Suspects on Train Turn Out to Be Musicians," *Boston Traveler*, 19 January 1950.

**Chapter Six Sidebar:
The Brink's Job**

1. *The Brink's Job*, production notes, press department, Universal Studios, 30 November 1978.
2. Clark Taylor, "Filming with the Men Who Broke the Brink's," *Los Angeles Times*, 4 June 1978.
3. Inter-Office Letter from William H. Sullivan, vice president of The Pittston Co., to Hendrik Hartong Jr., President and CEO of Brink's Inc., 9 May 1978.
4. Ibid.
5 "Filming with the Men Who Broke the Brink's."
6. *The Brink's Job*.
7. Ibid.

**Chapter Six Sidebar:
New Building Designs**

1. "Three Branches Move into New Homes," *Brink's Messenger*, Summer 1956.

**Chapter Six Sidebar:
Going Diesel**

1. "On the Go All Over U.S.," *Brink's Messenger*, Winter 1956.
2. C. W. Allen, "Two More King-Size Units Added to Brink's Fleet," *Brink's Messenger*, Spring 1958.
3. R. A. Seng and J. V. Gilmour, *Brink's—The Money Movers: The Story of a Century of Service*, (Chicago: Brink's Inc., 1959), 68.

Chapter Seven

1. Robert Andrews, Mary Biggs, and Michael Seidel, editors, *The Columbia World of Quotations*, (New York City: Columbia University Press, 2006).
2. "Brink's France: Historique," http://www.brinks.fr.
3. James L. Dunbar and Robert Grant Kingwell, *Bulletproof: A History of Armored Cars and the Colorful Characters Who Ran Them, Rode Them, and Sometimes Robbed Them*, (Hunt Valley, Maryland: Mid Atlantic Books & Journals, 2003), 320–321.
4. *Brink's Story Book 2004: Histoire de Brink's*, (France: Brink's France, 2003).
5. Scott Landry, interview by Jeffrey L. Rodengen, digital recording, 3 September 2008, Write Stuff Enterprises, Inc.
6. "Brink's Acquires Venezuelan Company," Brink's Inc. press release, 27 May 1970.
7. Brink's 1970 Annual Report.
8. *Bulletproof*, 309.
9. "Brink's Agrees to Form British Security Firm with MAT Transport, Ltd.," Brink's Inc. press release, 23 February 1972.
10. Brink's Inc. press release, 22 August 1972.
11. "Brink's Agrees to Form Australian Security Firm with Brambles Industries," Brink's Inc. press release, 13 January 1972.
12. *Brink's Story Book 2004*.
13. Erez Weiss, interview by Jeffrey L. Rodengen, digital recording, 9 September 2008, Write Stuff Enterprises, Inc.
14. "To Be Sure—Brink's It!," Brink's promotional pamphlet.
15. "Up Up and Away—with Brink's Air Courier Service," Brink's promotional pamphlet.
16. Ibid.
17. Ibid.
18. "To Be Sure—Brink's It!"
19. "Up Up and Away—with Brink's Air Courier Service."

20. Ibid.
21. Ibid.
22. Lynn Taylor, "Air Courier Service Secures Brink's Net," *Chicago Tribune*, 25 October 1970, C13.
23. Ibid.
24. "Brink's Wins Pact for Airport Cargoes," *Chicago Tribune*, 10 December 1971, C13.
25. "Air Courier Service Secures Brink's Net."
26. Leo Facenda, interview by Jeffrey L. Rodengen, digital recording, 12 November 2008, Write Stuff Enterprises, Inc.
27. "2 Arraigned in Hijacking of Jet Cargo," *Chicago Tribune*, 3 May 1967, B20.
28. "Brink's Courier Tells How He and Crew Foiled Hijack Attempt," *Chicago Tribune*, 16 September 1970, 1.
29. Robert Wiedrich, "Brink's Guard Is Seized on $71,000 Spree in West," *Chicago Tribune*, 25 May 1963, 1.
30. John O'Brien, "Brink's Guard Gets Leniency in Huge Theft," *Chicago Tribune*, 28 August 1963, A7.
31. Ibid.
32. John O'Brien, "It Was Goofy But I Enjoyed It: Embezzler," *Chicago Tribune*, 19 June 1963, A6.
33. "Brink's Guard Steps Out for a Drink," *Chicago Tribune*, 9 April 1960, 2.
34. "Brink's Driver Who Took $30,000 Gets Probation," *Chicago Tribune*, 2 June 1960, C15.
35. "Brink's Guard Steps Out for a Drink."
36. "Brink's Driver to Be Given Mental Test," *Chicago Tribune*, 12 April 1960, 19.
37. "CTA Re-elects Gunlock for 3-Year Term," *Chicago Tribune*, 7 September 1962, B8.
38. Patricia Leeds, "Police Rush Shotgun Orders," *Chicago Tribune*, 26 April 1968, 9.
39. "Parking Meter Jams Blamed on Brink's," *Chicago Daily News*, 24 November 1972.
40. "Parking Meters Stir Licensing Tiff Here," *Chicago Tribune*, 21 November 1972, 2.
41. "2 Clash at Parking Meter Hearings," *Chicago Tribune*, 22 November 1972, B2.
42. "Armored-Car Units of Baker Industries, Pittston Are Cited in Bid-Rigging Case," *The Wall Street Journal*, 22 June 1977.
43. "Three Brink's Aides Fined," *Chicago Tribune*, 13 November 1977, A16.
44. Brink's 1977 Annual Report.
45. "Three Brink's Aides Fined."
46. "Pay Hike Pact Averts Money Truck Strike," *Chicago Tribune*, 5 October 1965, A9.

47. "Strike Halts Armored Cars," *Chicago Tribune*, 9 June 1976, C10.
48. William Currie, "Guard Strike Brings Cash Jitters," *Chicago Tribune*, 10 June 1976, 3.
49. *Bulletproof*, 322.
50. *Bulletproof*, 290.
51. "Brink's Eyes Expansion to Meet Potential," *Chicago Tribune*, 26 April 1970, C13.
52. Ron Muir, interview by Jeffrey L. Rodengen, digital recording, 14 July 2008, Write Stuff Enterprises, Inc.
53. Frank Lennon, interview by Jeffrey L. Rodengen, digital recording, 15 May 2008, Write Stuff Enterprises, Inc.
54. "Brink's Plans to Buy More Shares and Announces Quarterly Dividend," Brink's Inc. press release, 14 August 1972.
55. *Bulletproof*, 334.

Chapter Seven Sidebar: Unusual Deliveries

1. R. A. Seng and J. V. Gilmour, *Brink's— The Money Movers: The Story of a Century of Service*, (Chicago: Brink's Inc., 1959), 17, 63–65.
2. Ibid., 63.
3. "Moon Surface Samples Distributed," NASA press release, 12 September 1969.
4. Greg Gittrich, "Cache of Gold Found at WTC," *New York Daily News*, 31 October 2001.
5. Brink's Museum display.
6. "KFC Secret Recipe Moved for Security Upgrade," Associated Press video, 10 September 2008.

Chapter Seven Sidebar: So Long, Chicago

1. James L. Dunbar and Robert Grant Kingwell, *Bulletproof: A History of Armored Cars and the Colorful Characters Who Ran Them, Rode Them, and Sometimes Robbed Them*, (Hunt Valley, Maryland: Mid Atlantic Book & Journals, 2003), 322–323.
2. Ibid., 322.

Chapter Eight

1. Michael Dan, interview by Jeffrey L. Rodengen, digital recording, 15 May 2008, Write Stuff Enterprises, Inc.
2. Jim Spurlock, interview by Jeffrey L. Rodengen, digital recording, 26 June 2008, Write Stuff Enterprises, Inc.
3. "Coal Stocks: Bleak Outlook," *New York Times*, 8 July 1983.
4. "Coal Industry Analysts' View," *New York Times*, 26 January 1984.

5. John Hague, interview by Jeffrey L. Rodengen, digital recording, 26 June 2008, Write Stuff Enterprises, Inc.
6. Michael Dan interview.
7. Gene Marcial, "Paul Douglas Has His Guard Up at Pittston," *BusinessWeek*, 27 June 1988.
8. John Hague interview.
9. Michael Dan interview.
10. *Brink's Link*, Fall 1986.
11. "Brink's Offers Rewards in Gold Theft," Associated Press, 10 July 1980.
12. "Ex-Guard Held in Theft of $1.85 Million in 1980," Associated Press, 23 November 1981.
13. "Hunt for Accused Thief in Brink's So Far Fruitless," Associated Press, 19 August 1980.
14. "Ex-Guard Pleads Guilty in Coast Brink's Robbery," *New York Times*, 10 February 1982.
15. "George Bosque; Guard Stole $1.85 Million," *Los Angeles Times*, 4 July 1991.
16. Ibid.
17. Ibid.
18. "Ex-Guard Pleads Guilty in Coast Brink's Robbery."
19. "George Bosque; Guard Stole $1.85 Million."
20. Jim Spurlock interview.
21. John Hague interview.
22. Michael Dan interview.
23. Ibid.
24. Krishna Kotak, interview by Jeffrey L. Rodengen, digital recording, 11 September 2008, Write Stuff Enterprises, Inc.
25. "Far East Part of Air Courier Growth," *Brink's Link*, Fall 1986, 4.
26. Ibid.
27. Ibid.
28. Joseph Eyal, interview by Jeffrey L. Rodengen, digital recording, 14 July 2008, Write Stuff Enterprises, Inc.
29. Marcia Simmons, "Brazil Investigating 'Loss' of $8 Million Sent from NY," *New York Times*, 22 February 1985.
30. Mary A. Uhlig, "Lost $8 Million Recovered After Arrest of 4 in Brazil," *New York Times*, 19 March 1988.
31. Thomas Gale Moore, "Trucking Deregulation," *The Concise Encyclopedia of Economics*, (Indianapolis, Library of Economics and Liberty, 1993).
32. "Trucking Deregulation."
33. Ibid.
34. Ibid.
35. Michael Dan interview.
36. Jeff Pagano, interview by Jeffrey L. Rodengen, digital recording, 6 November 2008, Write Stuff Enterprises, Inc.

37. Michael Dan interview.
38. James L. Dunbar and Robert Grant Kingwell, *Bulletproof: A History of Armored Cars and the Colorful Characters Who Ran Them, Rode Them, and Sometimes Robbed Them,* (Hunt Valley, Maryland: Mid Atlantic Books & Journals, 2003), 348–349.
39. Michael Dan interview.
40. "Speak Out Sessions Produce Good Results," *Brink's Link,* Fall 1985.
41. Michael Dan, "A Letter from the President," *Brink's Link,* Winter 1987.
42. Ibid.
43. "VGL Security devient Brink's–Nedlloyd," *Journal Pour le Transport International,* 9 September 1988.
44. *Brink's Link,* Winter 1989.
45. David Johnston, "Antitrust Lawyer Rises to Stardom Based on Combination of Caution and Zeal," *New York Times,* 6 November 1990.

**Chapter Eight Sidebar:
The Weather Underground Robbery**

1. Claudia Wallis, James Wilde, and Peter Staler, "Bullets from the Underground," *Time,* 2 November 1981.
2. Robert Worth, "Lines Are Drawn as 60s Radical Seeks Parole for an 80s Crime," *New York Times,* 20 August 2001.
3. Lisa W. Forderaro, "New Trial for Woman in 1981 Brink's Case Is Reopening Old Wounds," *New York Times,* 1 October 2006.
4. Larry Rohter, "60s Radicals Become Issue in Campaign of 2008," *New York Times,* 17 April 2008.
5. "New Trial for Woman in 1981 Brink's Case Is Reopening Old Wounds."
6. "Bullets from the Underground."
7. Ibid.
8. "Lines Are Drawn as 60s Radical Seeks Parole for an 80s Crime."

**Chapter Eight Sidebar:
Michael Dan**

1. Rhonda Brammer, "Brink's Is Unbound—And Is Ready to Roll—Freed from Its Legacy of Coal," *Barron's,* 28 November 2003.
2. Ibid.
3. Michael Dan, interview by Jeffrey L. Rodengen, digital recording, 15 May 2008, Write Stuff Enterprises, Inc.
4. Michael Dan interview.
5. Ibid.
6. Ibid.
7. Ibid.
8. Ibid.
9. Ibid.

Chapter Nine

1. Haim Zanzer, interview by Jeffrey L. Rodengen, digital recording, 13 November 2008, Write Stuff Enterprises, Inc.
2. Michael Dan, interview by Jeffrey L. Rodengen, digital recording, 15 May 2008, Write Stuff Enterprises, Inc.
3. Ibid.
4. "Pittston Announces Brink's European Acquisition," PR Newswire, 30 April 1990.
5. Joseph Eyal, interview by Jeffrey L. Rodengen, digital recording, 25 September 2008, Write Stuff Enterprises, Inc.
6. Erez Weiss, interview by Jeffrey L. Rodengen, digital recording, 9 September 2008, Write Stuff Enterprises, Inc.
7. Guy Bullen, interview by Jeffrey L. Rodengen, digital recording, 4 November 2008, Write Stuff Enterprises, Inc.
8. Michael Dan interview.
9. Haim Zanzer, interview by Jeffrey L. Rodengen, digital recording, 25 August 2008, Write Stuff Enterprises, Inc.
10. Kristina Chen, interview by Jeffrey L. Rodengen, digital recording, 3 September 2008, Write Stuff Enterprises, Inc.
11. Wynne Berry, interview by Jeffrey L. Rodengen, digital recording, 29 August 2008, Write Stuff Enterprises, Inc.
12. Joseph Eyal interview.
13. Greg Hanno, interview by Jeffrey L. Rodengen, digital recording, 26 June 2008, Write Stuff Enterprises, Inc.
14. "Brink's Provides Computerized Cash Management Services," Business Wire, 16 June 1997.
15. Bill Gunn, interview by Jeffrey L. Rodengen, digital recording, 11 November 2008, Write Stuff Enterprises, Inc.
16. Fred Purches, interview by Jeffrey L. Rodengen, digital recording, 26 June 2008, Write Stuff Enterprises, Inc.
17. Craig Wolf, "Bank Robberies Soaring Again, Baffling Bankers and the FBI," *New York Times,* 24 February 1990.
18. Gary Landry, interview by Jeffrey L. Rodengen, digital recording, 26 June 2008, Write Stuff Enterprises, Inc.
19. C. Buck Crebs, "Brink's Fulfills Search for Quality," *Brink's Link,* Winter 1994–95.
20. Pittston 1995 Annual Report.
21. Eleanor Wdovech, interview by Jeffrey L. Rodengen, digital recording, 18 November 2008, Write Stuff Enterprises, Inc.
22. Bill Vecchiarella, interview by Jeffrey L. Rodengen, digital recording, 4 November 2008, Write Stuff Enterprises, Inc.
23. Dennis Casteel, interview by Jeffrey L. Rodengen, digital recording, 27 June 2008, Write Stuff Enterprises, Inc.
24. Fred Meitin, interview by Jeffrey L. Rodengen, digital recording, 29 August 2008, Write Stuff Enterprises, Inc.
25. "Argentina Emerging as Biggest Brink's Start-Up," *Brink's Link Worldwide,* Fall 1997.
26. "Brink's Completes Acquisition of Venezuelan Affiliate," Business Wire, 16 January 1997.
27. "Brink's Acquires Balance of Netherlands Affiliate," Business Wire, 17 January 1997.
28. "Brink's and Zürcher Freilager Announce Creation of a Joint Venture to Serve Swiss Customers," Business Wire, 20 February 1997.
29. "Brink's Acquires Affiliate in France," PR Newswire, 27 January 1998.
30. "France: First Overseas Venture Acquired," *Brink's Link Worldwide,* Spring 1998.
31. Christian Berté, interview by Jeffrey L. Rodengen, digital recording, 7 October 2008, Write Stuff Enterprises, Inc.
32. "Brink's Incorporated Acquires Value of German Affiliate," PR Newswire, 4 June 1988.
33. "Affiliate with New Name Marks 25th Year," *Brink's Link Worldwide,* Fall 1998.
34. Tracy Heiner, interview by Jeffrey L. Rodengen, digital recording, 27 June 2008, Write Stuff Enterprises, Inc.
35. "Brink's Home Security Announces License Agreement," Business Wire, 21 July 1997.
36. "Brink's Home Security and DIRECTV Announce New Joint Marketing and Sales Agreement," PR Newswire, 4 February 1999.
37. Shellie Crandall, interview by Jeffrey L. Rodengen, digital recording, 26 June 2008, Write Stuff Enterprises, Inc.
38. Greg Hanno interview.

**Chapter Nine Sidebar:
Above and Beyond**

1. John Hague, interview by Jeffrey L. Rodengen, digital recording, 26 June 2008, Write Stuff Enterprises, Inc.

2. Gary Landry, interview by Jeffrey L. Rodengen, digital recording, 26 June 2008, Write Stuff Enterprises, Inc.

3. Ibid.

4. Jane Hamilton, interview by Jeffrey L. Rodengen, digital recording, 15 August 2008, Write Stuff Enterprises, Inc.

5. Yitzhak Rabin, interview by Jeffrey L. Rodengen, digital recording, 13 August 2008, Write Stuff Enterprises, Inc.

Chapter Ten

1. Jim Spurlock, interview by Jeffrey L. Rodengen, digital recording, 26 June 2008, Write Stuff Enterprises, Inc.

2. Bob Barrett, interview by Jeffrey L. Rodengen, digital recording, 11 November 2008, Write Stuff Enterprises, Inc.

3. Ibid.

4. Jenny Cole, interview by Jeffrey L. Rodengen, digital recording, 11 November 2008, Write Stuff Enterprises, Inc.

5. Ibid.

6. "Joseph Trombino: Close Calls Never Counted," *New York Times*, 17 September 2001.

7. Rhonda Brammer, "Brink's Is Unbound—and Is Ready to Roll— Freed from Its Legacy of Coal," *Barron's*, 28 November 2003.

8. Ibid.

9. "Brink's Inks Sale of Gas, Timber Operations," Associated Press, 21 July 2003.

10. "The Brink's Company Completes Sale of Coal Properties in West Virginia," Business Wire, 14 November 2003.

11. Chip Jones, "It Is Now Brink's on the NYSE," *Richmond Times-Dispatch*, 6 May 2003.

12. "Brink's Is Unbound—and Is Ready to Roll—Freed from Its Legacy of Coal."

13. Kelly Homan, "Brink's Unloads More Assets," *Daily Deal*, 22 July 2003.

14. "Brink's Sells Timber Operations," Associated Press, 31 December 2003.

15. "The Brink's Company Sells All of Its Shares of MPI Mines LTD Stock," Business Wire, 16 October 2003.

16. "The Brink's Company Reports Second Quarter Results," Business Wire, 31 July 2003.

17. Gary Landry, interview by Jeffrey L. Rodengen, digital recording, 26 June 2008, Write Stuff Enterprises, Inc.

18. "Brink's Is Unbound—and Is Ready to Roll—Freed from Its Legacy of Coal."

19. Michael Dan, interview by Jeffrey L. Rodengen, digital recording, 15 May 2008, Write Stuff Enterprises, Inc.

20. "The Brink's Company Reports Improved Second Quarter 2004 Preliminary Results," Business Wire, 4 August 2004.

21. Stephen Grocer, "Brink's Secures Shareholder Activities," *Mergers and Acquisitions Report*, 2 May 2005.

22. "The Brink's Company to Sell BAX Global for U.S. $1.1 Billion," PR Newswire, 16 November 2005.

23. Frank Lennon, interview by Jeffrey L. Rodengen, digital recording, 15 May 2008, Write Stuff Enterprises, Inc.

24. "The Brink's Company to Sell BAX Global for U.S. $1.1 Billion."

25. Michael Dan interview.

26. Ian Nunn, interview by Jeffrey L. Rodengen, digital recording, 27 June 2008, Write Stuff Enterprises, Inc.

27. "Brink's Inc. Agrees to Acquire Security Operations in Luxembourg and United Kingdom," Business Wire, 3 February 2005.

28. Carlo Weisen, interview by Jeffrey L. Rodengen, digital recording, 4 September 2008, Write Stuff Enterprises, Inc.

29. Ibid.

30. "Brink's Global Services to Increase Middle East Operations with a New Base at DMCC," Middle East Company Newswire, 2 January 2005.

31. "The Brink's Company Reports Higher Third-Quarter Earnings," PR Newswire, 1 November 2006.

32. Gabriel Allen, interview by Jeffrey L. Rodengen, digital recording, 21 August 2008, Write Stuff Enterprises, Inc.

33. Ibid.

34. "Brink's Brings Secure Document Destruction Home," PR Newswire, 18 May 2004.

35. Steve Bills, "Branching Out: Brink's to Enter Imaging Business," *American Banker*, 27 August 2004.

36. Steve Bills, "Brink's Captures New Partner in Metavante," *American Banker*, 21 May 2007.

37. "Brink's Launches Services to Help Companies Prevent Identity Theft," PR Newswire, 21 September 2005.

38. "Keep on Armored Truckin': Brink's Incorporated Is Bringing New Services to Retailers That Bring the Bank Closer to the Store," *Retail Merchandiser*, 1 March 2007.

39. "Brink's—Secure in Its Own Independence," *Mergers and Acquisitions Report*, 16 February 2004.

40. "Brink's Shares Climb After Shareholder Pushes for Consideration of Sale, Other Strategy," Associated Press, 18 December 2006.

41. "The Brink's Company to Spin-Off Brink's Home Security to Shareholders," PR Newswire, 25 February 2008.

42. Amit Zukerman, interview by Jeffrey L. Rodengen, digital recording, 26 September 2008, Write Stuff Enterprises, Inc.

43. David Gronow, interview by Jeffrey L. Rodengen, digital recording, 7 November 2008, Write Stuff Enterprises, Inc.

44. Ibid.

45. Gary Garton, interview by Jeffrey L. Rodengen, digital recording, 31 October 2008, Write Stuff Enterprises, Inc.

Chapter Ten Sidebar: A Fallen Hero

1. "Joseph Trombino: Close Calls Never Counted," *New York Times*, 17 September 2001.

2. John Muhlenforth, interview by Jeffrey L. Rodengen, digital recording, 11 November 2008, Write Stuff Enterprises, Inc.

3. Ibid.

4. Bob Barrett, interview by Jeffrey L. Rodengen, digital recording, 11 November 2008, Write Stuff Enterprises, Inc.

Chapter Ten Sidebar: Brink's and Technology

1. Guy Weissberg, interview by Jeffrey L. Rodengen, digital recording, 24 November 2008, Write Stuff Enterprises, Inc.

2. Jim Poteet, interview by Jeffrey L. Rodengen, digital recording, 17 July 2008, Write Stuff Enterprises, Inc.

3. Fred Purches, interview by Jeffrey L. Rodengen, digital recording, 26 June 2008, Write Stuff Enterprises, Inc.

INDEX

Page numbers in italics indicate photographs.